First Citizen

A Captivating Story Of Struggle, Resilience And Triumph

Favour Ezeifedi

Praise for THE FIRST CITIZEN

"A rich and compelling fictional biography, bringing Adannaya's journey to life with depth and cultural significance. This is as engaging as it is inspiring, blending tradition, resilience, and ambition in a way that will resonate with readers"

Jessie Raymond

The First Citizen

A Captivating Story Of Struggle, Resilience And Triumph

I hope this book inspires
you and brings joy to you

Favour

"Be Not Afraid of Greatness:
Some Are Born Great,
Some Achieve Greatness,
And Some Have Greatness
Thrust Upon Them"

William Shakespeare

This book is a fictional biography. All names, characters and incidents are the product of the author's imagination but based on actual events. Any resemblance to actual persons, living or dead is entirely coincidental.

ISBN: 978-1-0687803-7-0

Published in the United Kingdom in 2025 by

Framichi Publications.

www.framichipublications.com

Dedication

To my parents, who planted the seed of knowledge in my mind and nurtured it. Papa and Mama, thank you

To my daughter Nkem, who fills my heart with joy every day.

To my political mentor, the late Mike Jackson who saw the potential in me and took time to invest in me.

To God almighty. Indeed, the thoughts you have towards me are *thoughts* of peace and *not* of *evil*, to *give* me a **future** and a **hope.**

Acknowledgement

My deepest gratitude to everyone who encouraged me to write this book.

Thank you, Nkem Ezeifedi, Udoka Ezeifedi, Clifford Agugoesi, Helena Farrington, Sue Utting, and Sue Sleeman, for spending time reading parts of the manuscript and letting me see the characters through the sharp lenses of your eyes.

Thank you Casmir Ezeifedi , Udoka Ezeifedi ,Yohai Hakak and Sohail Bashir. You were there for me when it mattered most.

Finally, thanks to my publisher, Framichi Publications. Thank you for working tirelessly within my tight deadlines and making this book a reality.

PART ONE

Adannaya's Beginnings

CHAPTER 1

First Among Equals

Ten-year-old Adannaya Ugwumba held tightly to her father's hand as they walked home after another end-of-year prize-giving day at school.

Adannaya had just won the award for being the best student in her class once again, six years in a row. She beat all her classmates, both male and female students.

Adannaya was the only girl who beat all the boys in her class each year to achieve the first position across the subjects in her class. It was rare to have a student consistently staying at the top of the class every year of their academic journey, but Adannaya did it effortlessly to the pride of her family and community.

No one was prouder than her father, a former teacher with an academically gifted child he could boast about and celebrate. His nickname for her was Adam, which meant 'my beloved daughter'.

Her father walked majestically to his house, clutching Adannaya's award certificate and trophy in his left hand while holding his daughter's hand in his right. Chief Ugwumba burst into the house, beaming with pride and a huge grin on his face.

"Adam, go and call your mother for me. It is time for us to celebrate again."

"Yes Papa," Adannaya replied excitedly as she went looking for her mother.

As soon as his wife entered the living room, Chief Ugwumba said excitedly, "The most beautiful one! Adam has done it again o! I just attended the end-of-school-year awards ceremony at her school, and she won the best student of her class again," He announced, dancing around the room.

His wife smiled at him lovingly. She was used to it by now. Their first daughter, Adannaya, was always at the top of her class, and no one had ever beaten her to second place. It was no longer a surprise to her mother, but her husband danced every time it happened, as though it was the first time Adannaya had won an award.

"But my husband, you know Adannaya always comes first in her class," said his wife.

He stopped dancing to explain. "I know. I know, but this time, she won an extra award for being the only student in the school's history to win it consecutively every year for six years." He stretched his hands up to place the new trophy on the shelf along with the others Adannaya had won since she started primary school.

He stood there admiring all the trophies, which was the usual 'ritual' he performed every time Adannaya won a new trophy.

- Year 1 - Best Student Award
- Year 2 - Best Student Award
- Year 3 - Best Student Award
- Year 4 - Best Student Award
- Year 5 - Best Student Award
- Year 6 - Best Student Award

"Almighty God has blessed us with this intelligent child. We thank God." Mrs Ugwumba said, raising her hands up and looking at the ceiling as if God was there.

"Oh yes! Adam is a special blessing from God, and we must celebrate her success. Where is that big cockerel I bought yesterday? He asked as he completed his 'ritual' of admiring the trophies and sat in the living room.

"Another celebration? My husband, you know this is not good for our other children! When will you celebrate them too?" She pleaded. The Ugwumbas had six children in total, two boys and four girls. Adannaya was the first daughter and was aptly named with the prefix 'Ada,' meaning 'first daughter' in the Igbo language.

"I will celebrate them when they also study hard to come first place in their class." He looked at his wife disapprovingly for suggesting that. "Besides, you shower all your love on Akachi anyway."

His wife pretended not to hear that because she knew her first son was the apple of her eye. She dotted on him constantly, which was obvious to the rest of her family. Akachi could do no wrong in her eyes. Mrs Ugwumba saw Akachi as a comfort for the pain of losing her first baby (son) at birth. In traditional Igbo culture, having a male child secures a woman's place in her marriage and in-laws. Therefore, losing her first son was a traumatic experience early in her marriage, which led to her post-traumatic depression. The arrival of Akachi brought the much-needed healing that propelled her to become the amazon she was among her peers in the community.

She felt a little twinge of guilt every time this was raised, but a part of her felt she had to shower her love on Akachi since Adannaya got all the attention from her father and their extended family. She pressed on with the argument.

"You know you make them study hard too, so how can you imply they don't study hard enough?" She argued. Mrs Ugwumba was referring to her husband's strictness with their children's studies. He made them stop by his fashion shop on their way home from school every day so he could review their schoolwork for corrections and proper handwriting. This explains the similarity in the handwriting of all the children. Her thoughts were interrupted by her husband's continuation of the argument.

"Then where is the result? As a former teacher, all my children should be at the top of their class. After all, we are from a family of academicians. Remember, my younger brother is a secondary school principal, and my older brother is a head teacher. So, my children should all be equally brilliant, but only Adam is making her parents proud."

"But you know all our children cannot be the same. They have different strengths," Mrs Ugwumba continued.

"All I want is for our children to be at the top of their class. If Adam can do it, then why can't our other children do it?" He argued emphatically.

"You are right, my husband, but maybe we should not kill the chicken for Adannaya this time, Biko," She pleaded.

"Why not? Will the chicken not be eaten by all of us in this house? Is Adannaya going to eat it alone?" He asked with a knowing smile, like someone who knew he had won the argument.

"It is true. The whole family will eat the chicken together," She admitted with a grin.

"Ehe! Biko, go cook the chicken and remember to reserve the chicken thigh for our celebrant and first daughter. It is tradition," he added.

"I know," she agreed, laughing as she walked towards the kitchen to cook the celebratory meal. It was the same argument they had every time Adannaya won another school prize, and she wondered why she bothered arguing with her husband when she knew it always went his way.

Mrs Ugwumba opened the door to find a startled Adannaya and Akachi hiding behind the door where they had been eavesdropping on their parents' conversation.

"Don't you two have better things to do?" She scolded them. Akachi pushed Adannaya, and she stuck out her tongue at him.

"Stop it! Go to the kitchen now and start washing the vegetables for dinner."

The children ran excitedly to do their mother's bidding. Rice and chicken stew was on the menu, and it was their favourite meal.

Growing up in a typical patriarchal society, Adannaya relished breaking the status quo by beating all the boys to achieve first place in her class every year. The more she excelled at school, the more rewards, love, and attention she received from her family and community. Nigerian parents usually favoured the most academically intelligent child. Chief Ugwumba was no exception. He told her uncles and aunts about Adannaya's accomplishments, and they showered her with presents every time she came first in class. It put her in an admirable position in the family, and Adannaya loved it. She knew the importance of academic excellence in her young mind because it made her 'First Among Equals' at school, amongst her classmates and her community.

Her father had so much confidence in Adannaya's abilities that he introduced her to reading newspapers early on, and she became interested in current affairs. Daily Times was the newspaper of choice at that time, and Chief Ugwumba had a vendor who delivered it to his shop every day. He also subscribed to a monthly magazine for women known as Women's World for Adannaya to read.

Chief Ugwumba made Adannaya and her siblings watch the 9 pm news presented by the famous Frank Olizeh, the legendary newscaster who dominated the television airways in Nigeria at the time. After dinner every night, Chief Ugwumba made it mandatory for his children to watch the news. They all listened to the news with rapt attention because they knew Papa would ask them about it in the morning. It was an upbringing that

Adannaya would forever be grateful to her dear father for because it stood her in good stead for the future.

The time came for Adannaya to get into secondary school, and she gained admission into NdiOrlu Girls' College in the city, but her father did not want Adannaya to go to school in the city.

Chief Ugwumba was the son of parents who were entrepreneurs and owners of multiple businesses. He could see that his first daughter would be a trailblazer because she was so determined to succeed. She had a fighting spirit that needed to be harnessed. Therefore, he decided to send her to a place where she would learn leadership skills, resilience, and splendid work ethics.

He also wanted to shield Adannaya from the impact of the distractions studying in a big city would have on his first daughter. He believed firmly in the Igbo adage that says, "*if you raise the first daughter or son right, then the other children will be alright.*" This is based on the expectation and assumption that the first son or daughter would become a role model to her junior ones and can guide them accordingly.

Chief Ugwumba knew just the place to send his daughter for her secondary education, and it was the community secondary school in their village, NdiOkwara. Adannaya would have to live with his mother (Adannaya's grandmother), Lolo Obidiya Ugwumba.

The principal of the NdiOkwara community secondary school was Adannaya's uncle, who never failed to give her a present every time she came first in her class. Adannaya was happy to go to that school and live with her grandmother, who was always so nice to her.

Adannaya's grandmother lived in a large compound as the second of her grandfather's four wives. Like the other wives, her grandmother was industrious, running multiple businesses. Grandfather made provisions for his wives to be financially independent, which they loved. By helping her grandmother with business activities, Adannaya learnt many life lessons like hard work and business skills. She learnt to produce palm oil and became her grandmother's account clerk as she managed the payments received for her party rental business.

Adannaya also learned home values of respect and community spirit. Her grandmother taught her to look after those around her, and not just herself and her immediate family. A good example was when Adannaya swept her grandmother's compound or fetched water for her grandmother. Adannaya quickly learned that she had to do the same thing for the rest of the household. As a result, Ada would have to sweep the entire house and fetch water for the other three wives.

Adannaya's new busy schedule did not dampen her zeal for academic excellence. She continued to be at the top of her class and came first every year. None of her classmates could beat her, and she was elected as the senior prefect in the school.

After three years in the community secondary school, Adannaya's father brought her back to NdiOrlu city to complete her secondary school education at a different school. Chief Ugwumba made that decision because the standard of education had dropped considerably in the community school due to the relocation of their best teachers to the city. Her father was quite satisfied with all the values and life lessons Adannaya had learned in the village; therefore, there was no longer any reason for her to remain there.

When Adannaya returned to her family in NdiOrlu, she realised that schooling in the village was the best thing that her father did for her. She was more resilient, hardworking, and respectful.

Adannaya continued her secondary school education at a Technical College in NdiOrlu. It was a comprehensive school with both boys and girls. Her father made sure of that because he did not want Ada to attend a girls-only school. She started her fourth year of secondary school, and at the end of each term, she emerged in first place as usual.

Adannaya was like most teenage girls growing up in Nigeria at the time. They were all crazy about reading romance novels, and they could not get enough of them. The beautiful love stories made girls fantasise about the perfect boy and a great love.

Their favourite romance novels were the Pacesetters and Mills & Boon series of publications. They borrowed the books and exchanged them with one another. Reading those novels and hanging out with her friends was how Adannaya enjoyed her holidays, as they gave her a break from academic work. She went to the library regularly to borrow books to read. On her way home from the library, she would stop by her friends' home to hang out with them. On one of those trips back home from the library, she met the man who was to become her first love, and his name was Okey.

Okey Okafor rode his uncle's motorbike to the house. Okey spent his holidays with his maternal uncle, who lived near Adannaya's house. He was an undergraduate at the University of Benin and was home on holiday.

As he parked his motorbike in front of the house, he noticed pretty Adannaya, who was very well dressed in a beautiful Ankara print dress and strappy sandals. He stopped to observe her from a distance. She was sitting with his cousins, chatting and laughing. She was holding some books which she placed on her lap. She sat with her legs crossed and appeared visibly different from the other girls. She was decently dressed compared to his cousins, who had their legs and cleavages exposed. He liked that she was different, and he believed she must have been from an educated, good family background. Okey liked everything he saw and could not wait to be introduced.

When Adannaya was introduced to Okey, she was impressed that he was an undergraduate. She saw a handsome young man with a medium build, average height, and dark skin. He had a bubbly personality because he was cheerful and smiled all the time.

Adannaya liked him, and they chatted for a while. She left shortly after that, and every time she was on her way home from the library, she found Okey there with his cousins. It was obvious that he timed his visits to coincide with hers. He liked her more every time he saw her. He found her curiosity and eagerness to learn very refreshing. He could not believe how different she was because most girls her age were interested in getting married instead of planning for university and current affairs.

Okey got to know Adannaya, and a relationship blossomed between them naturally. He complimented her fashion style, and she told him it was all thanks to her father, who bought all his children's good clothes and continuously reminded them that *"you dress how you wish to be addressed."*

Okey found her fascinating. She was the only girl he knew who spent her allowance on newspapers and magazines. He could hold intelligent conversations with her about current affairs and other topics. Okey thought she was special, and he liked her a lot and supported her educational plans.

Adannaya was doing so well in year 4 that her school principal advised her father that Adannaya could sit the mock exams along with year 5 students. Her father was unsure about this and decided to ask his brother, Uncle Mazi, the school principal, for advice. This is why, in Africa, they say, *"it takes a village to raise a child."* Serious decisions about a child's future are usually taken collectively by the immediate and extended family.

Uncle Mazi said it was a clever idea, but Adannaya should take the Teacher Training Entrance Exam (TTC) because it is good for a woman to be a teacher. Adannaya also took the college of education entrance exam to enable her to become a secondary school teacher. However, she did it reluctantly because she was unhappy, and she wondered why no one had asked her brother Akachi to take the TTC exams to become a teacher. Adannaya did the exams all the same.

At the beginning of year five, her father bought her the JAMB (Joint Admission & Matriculation Board) exam forms for admission into the university. Adannaya had already received JAMB forms from her boyfriend, Okey. He bought it for her and travelled all the way from the University of Benin to NdiOrlu to bring them to her. She thought that was nice of him and liked him even more. The only problem was how to tell her father about it.

Fortunately for Adannaya, her father also bought her JAMB forms, which was a huge relief. It made her happy because she knew then that her father wanted more for her and would like her to go to university.

When all the exam results were released, it was no surprise to her family and school that Adannaya passed with flying colours. Adannaya was ecstatic. However, it was a bittersweet moment for her father; for a split second, he wished she had not passed the exams. The reason was because Akachi was in university and Chief

Ugwumba was already struggling to pay the tuition fees and support his son financially. Therefore, he was certain that he could not afford to pay for Adannaya's university education.

He tossed and turned all night as he wept with a mixture of gratitude and despondency over the dilemma he faced. He was tempted to send Adannaya to the College of Education for a diploma because it would be cheaper, but he knew that was the wrong thing to do because he knew his brilliant daughter deserved the best.

The next morning, Adannaya found her father sitting quietly by himself in the living room, lost in thought. She was worried about her father and what was going on in his mind.

"Good morning, Papa," Adannaya greeted her father.

"Adam, sit down," he beckoned.

"Ok Papa," She replied, as she sat beside her father.

Her father stared at her for a moment and said this empowering lgbo proverb, *"the God that gave the toad a big tuber of yam, will also give him the spade to dig it up."*

Adannaya looked at her father with a puzzled expression, waiting for an explanation of the proverb.

"What I am trying to say is this, the God that gave you this brilliant brain will provide the money for your university education." Adannaya nodded in understanding.

That proverb seemed to give Chief Ugwumba the motivation and determination he needed. He stood up and walked purposefully out of the house. Adannaya did not know where her father was going, but she was suddenly filled with unexplainable hope.

CHAPTER 2

A Special University Admission

When Chief Ugwumba left the house, he went to speak to his landlord. His brilliant plan was to sell his pick-up van to his landlord to raise the funds he needed to pay for Adannaya's university education.

This was a huge sacrifice because Chief Ugwumba needed that vehicle for his business activities. He had diversified into the distribution and logistics business, which could not be accomplished without a van, but he had resolved to hire a van whenever he needed one because his daughter's education was more important. Chief Ugwumba was an amazing father, one of the best.

Thankfully, his landlord agreed to buy the van, and Chief Ugwumba was able to reassure Adannaya that she would definitely be going to university and not the Teacher Training College or the College of Education.

Adannaya was over the moon because her dream was to become a professor and an accomplished academician. An excited Adannaya told her friends the good news that she would be going to university. She also informed her boyfriend, Okey, who was overjoyed at the good news.

Adannaya's mother was incredibly happy that her daughter was going to university. Since she had never attended high school, she was proud of her daughter's university admission. It meant so much to her. As a result, she was happy to sell her gold jewellery to help support her daughter's education.

Mrs Ugwumba was a community leader and someone other women in the community looked up to. She was jubilant and told everyone she knew in the community that her daughter had gained admission to university.

Adannaya applied to the University of Abuja to study for a bachelor's degree in English Linguistics. Although she passed her JAME (Joint Admission and Matriculation Examination) exam, she had to combine it with her WASCE (West African School Certificate Examination) result to be accepted into the University. As a result of the WAEC schedule, Adannaya's WASCE result was not due to be released before her university was scheduled to commence the new school year.

Adannaya was worried that her dream of a university education may be delayed. Will the University insist that she must wait until her WAEC results were released? Would it mean she would lose this admission and retake the JAMB exam? Would they keep her place open until her results were released?

Adannaya discussed these concerns with her parents, and they encouraged her to pray and remain optimistic because they had to believe everything would work out as planned. Her mother bought her a beautiful suitcase and helped her pack up her luggage for the trip to the university.

The next day, her dad took her to Onitsha, where the bus station was located, and paid for her journey. He was holding onto his belief in that proverb about the 'toad and the big tuber of yam.' It was his trust in God that the issue with Adannaya's university education would be resolved.

In addition, Chief Ugwumba also had absolute faith in God and his clever daughter, and he sent her off to Abuja with confidence that Adannaya could handle the situation and get herself accepted at the university.

Adannaya boarded one of the most popular choices of travel, known as a 'luxurious bus ' by one of the major transport companies to Abuja, 'The Young Shall Grow.' They were often the commuter buses of choice for those travelling long distance to various parts of Nigeria.

The journey took the entire day, and Adannaya arrived in Abuja at night. She met a kind woman on the coach who took her to one of her extended relations at Abuja. In the morning, Adannaya went to the university.

At the admissions office, she explained to the officers that she was still waiting for her WAEC result and that she had her mock exam certificate with her. When Admission Officers saw her excellent grades, the university accepted Adannaya's mock result and allowed her to register for her course pending the release of her WAEC result. Based on the Nigerian annual exam calendar, the result was due in a few weeks, just before the university matriculation.

That was how Adannaya solved that worrisome problem. Her hard work and academic excellence had always made her special and kept her at the top of every class; that had once again made a difference and enabled her into university under incredibly unique circumstances.

As the university expected, Adannaya's WAEC result was released before matriculation, and she passed the exam with flying colours. She was finally able to relax and start enjoying her new life at university. She wrote to her parents, and they were glad and relieved to hear that Adannaya was settled at university, just like her father knew she would be.

Adannaya chose to study at the University of Abuja, out of all the universities in the country, because she wanted to experience a culture different from the Igbo culture she was born into and had known all her life. She wasn't wrong about that because the university was full of students from very varied cultures. There were Hausas, Yorubas, Efiks, Edos, Urhobos, Ijaws, Itsekiris, Fulanis, etc. Adannaya loved it and made many friends.

At the age of sixteen she was one of the youngest and most focused in her class. Adannaya stood out, and many were drawn to her. Her classmates were either teasing her or treating her like a younger sister. It was no surprise that she made friends easily. Her closest friend was a Yoruba girl named Shade. She was a bit older than Adannaya, took her under her wing and looked after her, and they became lifelong friends.

Adannaya deepened her Christian faith through the Christian Student Fellowship (CSF). She joined the fellowship and became a devout believer. It became a part of who she was as a person, and it began to reflect in her letters to her parents. Adannya's father described them as very soothing and comforting as they reflected her deep conviction in her relationship with God and His love.

The beautiful love affair between Okey and Adannaya continued to blossom. Since they were miles apart from each other (University of Abuja to University of Benin), they resorted to writing love letters to each other. There were no mobile phones in Nigeria then. Therefore, writing love letters to each other was the best medium for communicating and staying in touch, except when they were home on school holidays and could see each other and spend much time together.

Adannaya had a close relationship with her father and knew she could tell him anything. Besides, she had made a promise to him that she would inform him when she was beginning to have a meaningful relationship. Adannaya decided the time had come since she and Okey were deeply in love with each other.

Adannaya waited until her father was sitting alone in the living room one evening, and she went to sit beside him.

"Papa, there is a boy called Okey who likes me, and I like him, too. He is the boy that comes to our neighbour, Okafor's house."

"I know him. He is that young man who rides his uncle's motorbike. He greets me whenever he sees me." Chief Ugwumba nodded.

"Okey is an undergraduate and the type of person you like. He is intelligent. I am sure you will like him, Papa."

Adannaya was expecting words of approval from her father because she was so certain that he would like Okey. Instead, all her father did was mumble.

"Hmmm…"

Adannaya knew that wasn't a good sign. "Papa, why did you say hmmm...?"

"My daughter, before you get into a serious relationship with a man, you must look at his parents and seek to know their values."

"But why do you say that, Papa?"

"Because if their values do not align with yours, you should not marry their son."

"What is wrong with Okey's parents?" Adannaya asked because she did not understand what her father was alluding to.

"Have you seen his parents? Be careful, Adam."

"But Papa…."

Her father raised a finger to his lips to stop her. "They say a word is enough for the wise, and I believe that I raised a wise daughter. There is nothing more to say."

"Ok, Papa," she replied. Adannaya knew that was the end of the conversation, so she walked out of the house. She needed to clear her head. Disapproval of her relationship was the last thing Adannaya expected from her father because Okey seemed to tick many boxes of the type of man her father would want her to marry.

Adannaya was so in love with Okey that she did not let her father's opinion come between them. She decided to say nothing about this to Okey and continued as if her conversation with her father had never happened.

The rumours about her relationship with Okey started to spread in their community, and Adannaya's mother heard about it. One day, Adannaya visited Okey as usual. He sat at the table in his room with an open newspaper in front of him while Adannaya lay on the bed. The fan was blowing cool air around the humid room, and the lovers relaxed and chatted happily. They were not doing anything wrong neither were they in a compromising position, so they left the door ajar.

To Adannaya's astonishment, her mother burst into the room. Mrs Ugwumba was so angry to see her teenage daughter alone with a boy in his room and lying on his bed. She screamed at Adannaya and dragged her out of the bed.

"What are you doing here, eh? I said what are you doing here, you foolish girl" She slapped Adannaya twice on both cheeks.

"Mama! Mama, I did not do anything wrong," Adannaya tried to explain as the tears rolled down her cheeks.

"Shut up and follow me right now."

Okey recovered from the shock and leapt up from his chair, but he did not know what to do to help his girlfriend.

Mrs Ugwumba dragged her daughter outside and beat her up thoroughly. Then she spat on the floor and pointed at it.

"Before this spit dries up, you had better be back at home." Then she got on her motorbike and drove away.

Okey was shocked beyond words. He tried to console Adannaya and advised her to go home before her mother got there to avoid being beaten up once again. Adannaya knew he was right, so she ran home.

Mrs Ugwumba rode straightaway to her husband's shop to tell him what happened. Chief Ugwumba did not like what he heard Adannaya got up to. He needed to talk some sense into his daughter.

As soon as he arrived home, Chief Ugwumba summoned Adannaya for a serious talk. Adannaya noticed that her father did not bother to remove his Ndi Nze cap, which was the first thing he did when he came home. She realised how serious this matter was.

"What were you doing in that boy's room?" asked her father angrily.

"I was not doing anything with him, but Mama embarrassed me. The door was slightly open; she just pushed it, and it opened. Ask Mama if she saw me doing anything."

"I have always told you that you should never put yourself in a position where people will make insinuations about you, and you will have to explain. Remember that perception is everything, especially for a girl. I have told you this over and over again," he said emphatically.

"Yes, Papa," Adannaya listened quietly.

"In any case, I am going to have a word with that young man," said her father.

"Ah, Papa!" Adannaya started to panic inwardly. She did not want her father to scare Okey off and make matters worse.

"I am going to make it clear to him that he cannot mess with my daughter!"

"But Papa, I did not do anything with him! I am not that type of girl, Papa" She tried to reassure her father. Adannaya was right because she was still a virgin.

However, Chief Ugwumba's mind was made up. As a devout Catholic, he considered it his duty to prevent his daughter from having sex before marriage and the risk of unplanned pregnancy. He kept his word and had that important conversation with Okey.

Adannaya thought that was the end of her relationship woes and she stayed away from Okey to avoid any more trouble from her parents.

Unfortunately, that was not the end of the matter. The news that she was beaten up by her mother and dragged away from Okey's house spread quickly around their community like wildfire. As with all stories that get retold by those who did not witness it, they began to embellish the story. When Okey's mother eventually heard about the incident, she was told that Adannaya's mother went to her brother's house and beat up Adannaya and Okey as well. As they say in Nigeria, the grapevine had 'added salt and pepper to the story.' Unsurprisingly, Okey's mother was offended by it and decided to pay the Ugwumbas a visit.

Okey's mother, Mrs Okafor, was ready for a fight, so the moment she stepped into the home of the Ugwumbas, she started shouting at Adannaya's mother.

"You should keep that daughter of yours in your house because she is the one running after my son. Okey did not come looking for her; she was the one who came looking for him. So, keep her away from my son and leave my son alone o!"

That was her message, and after she delivered it, Mrs Okafor departed without waiting for a response from Mrs Ugwumba. The situation became too messy and overblown. Both parents disapproved of the relationship. It was impossible for the lovers to convince their parents otherwise. After this incident, Adannaya and Okey decided to stay away from each other when they were home on holiday.

This reaction by the parents to their children's relationship was the norm in typical Nigerian families then. The parents never allowed their daughters to date anyone. They would prefer to hear marriage proposals and not necessarily relationships. The fact that Chief Ugwumba asked Adannaya to inform him when she had a meaningful relationship with a boy made him one of the most progressive parents of his time.

The advantage the lovers had in their relationship was that they were both undergraduates in faraway universities, so they were able to stay connected and occasionally visited each other without their parents knowing about it.

At this point, Adannaya began to have many suitors, mainly rich traders from her Igbo tribe. They came to indicate their desire to marry Adannaya by bringing a bottle of whiskey to her father. They were not very educated men but wanted an educated 'trophy' wife to boast about and improve their social standing in the community. The fact that Adannaya was a high achiever only made her more eligible and desirable to them.

The whole community knew her as the girl who always came first in her class in school. The one who could never be beaten to second place. It made her a little legend. These rich Igbo traders hardly knew Adannaya as a person, which was why their marriage intention was not necessarily about love or fondness, and her father knew that.

Chief Ugwumba accepted the gifts from them but informed them that his daughter could not discuss marriage intentions until after her graduation from university. Adannaya was not interested in any of her suitors because she did not want to marry an Igbo trader.

When Okey learned about Adannaya's many suitors, it made him feel insecure. He also felt threatened by Adannaya's strong intellectual sagacity as Adannaya continued to progress at the University. Who could blame him? After all, Adannaya's parents disapproved of their relationship, so he believed they were likely to accept one of those suitors. Luckily for Okey, Adannaya only had eyes for him, but that did not stop him from feeling apprehensive about her many suitors.

Okey graduated from the University of Benin and was posted to Abuja for his National Youth Service(-NYSC). It was fate that brought him to Abuja, although many assumed he used some connections at the NYSC headquarters to influence his posting to Abuja so he could stay close to Adannaya. Okey did nothing like that. The lovers had the opportunity to live in the same city and spend as much time together as possible.

Okey knew that he had no future with Adannaya. He loved her, but he knew their parents would never approve of their relationship. He knew Adannaya loved him very much and was determined to stick with him with the belief and hope that their parents would eventually change their minds and give their blessing. Okey could not end his relationship with Adannaya, so he came up with a strategy to 'push' her away so she would dump him.

Shortly after, Adannaya noticed Okey was dating different girls in Abuja and back home in NdiOrlu. It bothered Adannaya, but every time she confronted Okey, he denied it. She was hurt by his cheating and was beginning to lose interest in the relationship.

After his National Youth Service, Okey was retained by the company in an excellent role.

Upon reflection, Adannaya wondered if it was the fiery opposition to their relationship that made Okey take the steps he did or his insecurities around her. Adannaya was also intellectually strong, and Okey felt intimidated. Adannaya had to accept that it was over and that there was no future for them both, and that was the end of their five-year relationship.

Adannaya graduated from the university and was posted to Potiskum in Borno state for her National Youth Service. In her usual curious and studious manner, she did some research to find out all she could about the NYSC.

Adannaya was excited about undergoing her one-year service for her country. It was also another adventure for her and a chance to live within a different culture, among the Hausa and Fulani people of Northern Nigeria.

Adannaya was assigned to teach the English language at a Teacher's College in Potiskum. She was given accommodation at the Youth Corper's Quarters, a building that was donated to NYSC by the owner, Major General Bomai. It was located beside the Major's residence and family home. It was a nice house, and Adannaya shared her flat with two other female corps members. Once again, she was the youngest in the group of corpers and the only one who taught English.

The son of the Major was a Brigadier in the army. He was stationed at Ibadan and only came home to Potiskum when he was on annual leave. His name was Yusuf, and he was an incredibly handsome young man, tall, dark, muscular, and handsome, with dimples on both cheeks. He made women swoon, and they hung around him like flies to a light. He was the most eligible bachelor in Potiskum, and all the young women had their eyes and hearts set on him.

Yusuf liked to hang out at the corpers lodge chatting with the corpers. Adannaya and her two female flatmates enjoyed his company, but he was more interested in Adannaya, whom he found incredibly smart and young to be a university graduate.

One day, during one of their many chats, they started talking about Ibadan, where Yusuf was stationed. Adannaya mentioned that her uncle was the owner of a well-known pharmacy store at New Market Road in the city. Yusuf knew the store and was surprisingly glad to know that little information, but Adannaya did not notice it then.

Adannaya and Yusuf spent many late nights talking, and it was clear that he enjoyed her company, but he did not ask to date her. They continued to be mere friends; that was all Adannaya believed they were. She found him attractive and good company but had no romantic intentions towards him.

Yusuf liked Adannaya very much and believed she would make a good wife. He felt they had a special connection because they could talk for hours, which he found rare in most of the women he interacted with. He was convinced that she liked him too because she spent so much time in his company. However, instead of making his feelings known to Adannaya, he decided to visit her uncle in Ibadan to discuss his intentions for her.

Yusuf stormed Adannaya's uncle's shop in a convoy of cars with his army friends, and they caused terrible traffic. He brought the street to a standstill. Adannaya's uncle was surprised to receive a visit from an army officer. He soon found out the reason for the visit.

"Good afternoon, sir," greeted Yusuf.

"Good afternoon. Who are you?"

"I am Brigadier Yusuf Bomai. I met your daughter, who is serving in Potiskum, and she said you are like a father to her."

"Yes, my brother's daughter is serving there." Uncle Ekwueme nodded.

"I really like Adannaya, and I have come to ask for her hand in marriage," Yusuf explained.

"Really?" Uncle Ekwueme could not hide his surprise.

"Yes sir."

Uncle Ekwueme was not expecting that, and before he could say anything anymore, Yusuf beckoned to his boys, and they brought the gifts out of all the car boots. There were bags of rice, beans and yams, bottles of wine and spirits. It was a large quantity of gifts.

Uncle Ekwueme was surprised at the lavish gifts and the convoy of vehicles because it was such a spectacular sight. His customers and employees at the shop kept asking him what was going on and who the army officers were. All he could do was shrug his shoulders and wait for Yusuf to finish supervising the offloading of the gifts so they could resume the conversation.

"I just want to do the needful."

"Have you discussed this with Adannaya? Have you asked her?"

"Not yet, but I want to get your permission first because we both live in the same town. If you give me the permission, I will pay the bride price and take care of everything in the blink of an eye."

Uncle Ekwueme had to laugh at his enthusiasm and eagerness. "Well, you know I am not her father, so I will talk to her father and ask Adannaya herself. We have to discuss it with our kinsmen before I can give you an answer."

"But she told me you are like a father to her."

"I know that, but she has a father, and her father's permission is what you need, so let me talk to her father. I will inform him and also write to Adannaya about it."

"Ok, thank you sir," answered a satisfied Yusuf. He drove away feeling confident that he had impressed Adannaya's family and blown them away with his visit and lavish gifts. They could not refuse him now, he thought.

Uncle Ekwueme had no intention of getting Chief Ugwumbas permission. He did write to inform Adannaya's father, but it was not in favour of Yusuf because he knew already that marrying a Muslim who was likely to have up to four wives eventually would be a difficult marriage. He also wrote to Adannaya to ask her what was happening.

When Yusuf returned a week later for an answer, Uncle Ekwueme gave him the same response as last time, that he was still discussing the proposal with the rest of their family. Yusuf eventually figured out that it was delaying tactics and that his proposal would not be accepted, so he reluctantly stopped visiting Adannaya's uncle.

The letter that Adannaya received from her uncle was an angry one asking her if she had lost her mind to consider marrying a Muslim man. 'Do you want to be one of four wives?' He wrote. From the letter, it was clear that the whole family was appalled to receive such a marriage proposal for Adannaya.

Not only was she surprised to receive that letter, but she was also mad at Yusuf. How could he propose marriage to her family without talking to her first? What was he thinking, and more importantly, why did he expect her to marry him when they were not even in a relationship? It was ridiculous. Adannaya was waiting impatiently for Yusuf to return to Potiskum so she could confront him.

A few months later, when Yusuf finally came home for another break from work, Adannaya immediately raised the issue with him. Yusuf explained why he took that step, and Adannaya got the full picture. A part of her was flattered that the most eligible bachelor in Potiskum chose her and wanted to marry her, but she never admitted that thought.

Adannaya tried to be understanding and let Yusuf down gently. She explained that the major obstacle was that she did not want to end up as one of his many wives.

Yusuf argued that he would not marry another wife after her, but Adannaya did not believe him because Yusuf's father had four wives.

Lastly, she could hear her father's voice loud and clear in her ears as though he was standing beside her, which was, "before you get into a serious relationship with a man, you should look at his parents and seek to know their values."

It made sense to Adannaya in this situation because she knew Yusuf's father, and she could see that he was the wrong man for her. Yusuf accepted the rejection graciously, and they maintained their friendship until the conclusion of Adannaya's youth service and her subsequent departure from Potiskum.

CHAPTER 3

A New World

When the end of the National Youth Service is approaching, every Nigerian youth corper starts to contemplate their future job prospects. Those who end up in a good organisation for their youth service wish and pray to be retained and offered permanent employment.

Adannaya found herself in that position. She did not want a career in the teaching profession like her father and uncles wanted, but she was unsure of the career she wanted and was still trying to figure it out. She also knew she did not want to live and work in Northern Nigeria, where she had her university education and Youth Service. NdiOrlu in Eastern Nigeria was where she was born and lived all her life. Therefore, she decided it was time to experience Western Nigeria, and she chose Lagos because of the amazing things she had heard about it.

Lagos was the commercial nerve centre of Nigeria. The biggest and best companies were located in Lagos, and there were many of them. This apparently meant there would be better job opportunities in Lagos. It was no surprise then that Adannaya set her sights on Lagos. However, there were a few hurdles she had to overcome before she could move there.

Where would she stay? How would her parents and family welcome the news of her move to Lagos? How would she navigate the complexity of finding a job in Lagos based on the stories of the difficulties faced by graduates in Nigeria and the fact that it took a year or two for most of them to find jobs?

Maybe it was Adannaya's characteristic determination and resilience, but she had a hunch that her experience would be different and positive. She knew she had to plan everything carefully to give herself a good start, at least.

Adannaya wasted no time in making plans for her move to Lagos before the completion of her Youth Service. She knew she needed a place to stay until she found a job and attained some financial stability. To that end, Adannaya wrote to her favourite aunt in Lagos to ask for her support in this regard. Auntie Nkechi was her mother's sister and a kind woman. Thankfully, her aunt was happy for Adannaya to live with her for as long as she needed to. With that problem solved, Adannaya prepared to tackle the next problem, breaking the news to her parents.

Adannaya returned home after her Youth Service to a warm welcome from her family. There was another celebration with the biggest cockerel in their poultry. Her parents were proud of their first daughter, the graduate. They knew her next step was seeking employment and building a career, but they did not rush Adannaya because they trusted her to make those decisions herself.

After a week at home, Adannaya decided it was time to discuss her career plans with her parents. She knew her parents would be worried that she was embarking on a journey into the difficult territory of job hunting in Nigeria, but Adannaya had a trump card she was going to use to convince them and allay their fears. After dinner one evening, she asked for a private chat with them.

"Papa and Mama, I have decided to move to Lagos to find a job," Adannaya stated. As expected, her mother was alarmed and the first to react.

"How can you move all the way to Lagos to find work when we live in a big city like NdiOrlu?"

"The most beautiful. Let Adam finish telling us her plans. I am sure she has her reasons," said her father.

"But why does she have to move so far away from home and her family? Adannaya, have you applied for any jobs here?" Mrs Ugwumba asked her daughter.

"No, mama. It is not that I don't want to work in NdiOrlu; it is just that Lagos is a bigger city with more opportunities, she said quietly. Adannaya was expecting this reaction from her mother, so she was prepared to listen patiently and try to convince them.

Before her mother could respond, her father interjected once again. 'Let us wait for our daughter to finish.' We raised an intelligent child and had to listen to her entire plan. Mrs Ugwumba nodded reluctantly, but she listened to her husband this time and calmed down.

This was Adannaya's cue, and she explained why she chose Lagos to start her career and that it was purely based on job prospects. She convinced her parents that it was the perfect place for someone like her who was still unsure about the profession she wanted.

Her parents began to understand the reasons for her decision, but they stll had their reservations.

"But where will you stay in Lagos? I hear accommodation is extremely expensive there," asked her mother.

"Mama, I wrote to Aunty Nkechi, and she said I can stay with her for as long as I want."

"Thank God for that," sighed her father. Her mother wasn't satisfied with that, though.

"But Nkechi lives in a house with so many people. You know she is one of four wives, and they all live together in the same house. How will you cope with that?"

"Let her go and stay with them. She will be able to adapt. You know our daughter is resilient," Chief Ugwumba said to his wife reassuringly.

A relieved Adannaya said, "Thank you, Papa. Thank you, Mama."

Her father nodded, and after a brief pause, he asked another question that Adannaya was expecting.

"But Lagos is very rough. How will you find work there? Do you know what to do?" His voice was laced concern once again.

"My good friend from university is working in Lagos already, and she promised to help me find a job over there," answered Adannaya confidently.

That pleased her mother. "Ah! I am happy to hear that. Go in peace then, my daughter!"

Adannaya leaned over to hug her mother. "I will, Mama." Her mother hugged her back tightly.

"What are we even worried about when your brother, Obioma, is in Lagos," said her father.

"But Obioma is an apprentice. Adannaya cannot depend on him yet," argued her mother.

"I know, but at least she will have more family over there in case of any problem."

"That is true, Papa, but I will be fine, and there won't be any problem."

"I have faith in you, my dear daughter, but promise me one thing. If you do not find a job after one year, you must return home to NdiOrlu, and we will help you find work here," said her father emphatically.

"But why won't I find work after such a long time, Papa?"

"Because I hear some graduates do not find a job until after one or two years," answered her father.

"Yes, I have heard that too, but it is not my portion in Jesus' name," said Adannaya as she made the sign of the cross on her forehead.

"Mba! God forbid! It will not be our daughter's portion o!" Her mother said as she snapped her fingers over her head. It was a superstitious way of warding off dreadful things in Igbo culture.

"Let us pray for her and give her our blessing," said her father. Adannaya knelt down, and her parents placed both their right hands on her head and prayed for several minutes, asking God to protect their daughter and grant her a successful career in Lagos.

A happy and very relieved Adannaya left for Lagos a few days later. She had saved some money from the wages she received during her year-long National Youth Service in Potiskum. She did not want to ask her parents for money anymore, nor did she want to bother Aunty Nkechi with such issues in Lagos. Adannaya did not want to be a burden to anyone now that she was a graduate. Her savings were enough to pay for her journey to Lagos and job search expenses. So, she believed anyway.

Adannaya boarded her favourite bus line, 'The Young Shall Grow' company. She had two novels *(Second Class Citizen and The Beautiful Ones Are Not Yet Born)* on her to read on the long journey because she knew it would last the entire day. However, she found her mind drifting to the amazing things her research revealed about Lagos. It filled her with excited anticipation, and she couldn't wait to get there.

Lagos is located in southwestern Nigeria, and it was the capital of Nigeria. Although a part of Yorubaland and fondly named Eko by the Yorubas, Lagos was the most multicultural city in Nigeria. This was because most Nigerians who sought the best business or job opportunities lived in Lagos.

The city was the centre of commerce, entertainment, technology, education, politics, fashion, art, and tourism in Nigeria. The most important 'players' in these sectors were in Lagos. For politics, it was the seat of the federal government. In entertainment, the best musicians and movie stars lived in Lagos. Most international investors had their base in Lagos, which was the main attraction for tourists because the city was blessed with exceptionally beautiful sandy beaches. The Lagos seaport was one of the largest in Africa. That explained the huge population of over ten million at the time and why Lagos is considered a megacity and the most populous urban landscape in Africa.

Lagos is divided into a mainland and an island. The best part of the mainland is Ikeja, the administrative headquarters for Lagos state. The island is the most beautiful part of the city, with the best roads and architecture. It was the most affluent and exclusive area of Lagos and the favourite place for white foreigners and tourists. Known as Victoria Island and Ikoyi, the island was the most sought-after location by the rich and mighty. There is a saying that Lagos is a city where the rich and poor live side by side. There are ghettos in Lagos, such as the Maroko area, which is adjacent to Victoria Island and Ikoyi.

Adannaya arrived in Lagos at night. Her first impression of Lagos was the terribly slow-moving traffic and the loud voices of bus conductors shouting to passengers as they drove as fast as the traffic would allow. The streets were full of pedestrians walking up and down clutching their luggage and work tools. Adannaya had never seen such a crowd on a street at the same time. It was a populous city indeed. She was thankful for her seat by the coach window as it enabled her to have a glimpse of the city.

There were passengers rushing to get on buses that were still moving. Even when the bus stopped, no one queued up. They simply pushed each other and fought their way into the bus. She noticed the huge yellow and black vehicle that looked like a cross between a bus and a lorry. It was quite an ugly and unsafe-looking monstrosity. Why would anyone board a vehicle like that, she wondered as passengers fought to get on board.

Adannaya also noticed the hawking of food items on the road. There were bread sellers, a bunch of plantains, pastries, and various snacks. They shoved their products at all the car occupants in the traffic and promoted their goods as quickly as possible. Adannaya was amazed that business could be conducted this way. It was risky on so many levels. When she saw a passenger accept a loaf of bread and drive off without paying, Adannaya was not surprised.

The angry hawker ran after the vehicle, screaming in pidgin English, "Pay me my money o! Pay me my money!" He said repeatedly until the car disappeared into the distance. He gave up and stopped running. He cursed at one of the occupants of the departed car for not paying for the bread.

"Ko ni da fun e. E no go beta for you. Your papa and your mama!" He was only a teenager, and he cursed in frustration, almost in tears. Surprisingly, he hurriedly approached another vehicle and tried to sell another loaf of bread.

Adannaya was perplexed. Why did the hawker continue to make the same mistake with the hope of a different and better outcome? She could not understand it, but it was definitely fascinating to watch. Adannaya noticed another hawker who received payment from a vehicle driver for a bunch of plantain. She promised to bring back his change, and he waited for her in the traffic, but she never returned with the change. He had to drive off when the cars behind him started blaring their horns. A few minutes later, she emerged laughing and applauding herself for tricking a customer. "God catch one for me today," she said to her fellow hawkers, and they all laughed. Adannaya concluded that there must be laws for trading in Lagos traffic and wondered what they were.

Lagos was going to be an interesting place to live; Adannaya could feel it. She was enjoying the spectacle and knew she could watch this the whole night, but she was also exhausted from the long journey. Just then, the coach stopped, and the driver announced that it was the end of the journey. Adannaya hurried off the coach to the waiting arms of her dear aunt, who was waiting for her at the station. Aunty Nkechi gave her a nice hug and congratulated her on her graduation. She was as beautiful as ever, tall and slim with an eye-catching figure. She looked so elegant in her white linen dress.

They exchanged pleasantries, and her aunt's driver put Adannaya's luggage in the boot. As they drove off towards her aunt's home in Surulere, Adannaya could not contain her excitement. She had so many questions about Lagos life and tried to ask them all at once. Her aunt laughingly calmed her down and tried to answer all her questions. She told Adannaya that the ugly yellow bus was called a 'molue' and it was the cheapest form of transportation in Lagos, so she advised Adannaya to use it if she wanted to minimise her expenses while job hunting. Adannaya nodded, but inwardly, she vowed never to get on a *molue*.

Adannaya told her aunt about the hawkers, and Auntie Nkechi laughed at the puzzled frown on her face. "My dear, they say you can buy everything you need to cook a pot of soup on Lagos traffic. If there are any laws, no one obeys them or ensures they are obeyed. That is Lagos for you," explained Auntie Nkechi, giggling once more at the astonished look on Adannaya's face.

They arrived at Aunty Nkechi's home, a large two-storey building divided into four flats. It was a polygamous household of a wealthy man where Adannaya met the other three wives and all the children, including Aunty Nkechi's four children. It was a boisterous family house with children running around and making plenty of noise. Adannaya remembered her experience in the village when she lived with her grandmother. It was a similar polygamous family setting, and Adannaya realised that her experience with her grandmother had prepared her for this new life at her aunt's home. She knew exactly how to fit in, and it was going to be okay.

Two days after arriving in Lagos, Adannaya contacted Shade. She was her best friend at university and would give her the guidance and support she needed to find employment. Shade worked at the Sentinel Newspapers, a daily newspaper that published job vacancies in the newspaper every Tuesday. Everyone called it the Tuesday Sentinel, and jobseekers waited anxiously for that publication to hit the newsstands. This put Shade at a vantage position to learn about new job opportunities before they hit the newsstands. She told Adannaya about the best jobs that were most suitable to her qualifications and work experience before the publication. With this information, Adannaya was able to prepare her job application for submission ahead of other applicants.

Shade helped her create a good CV and taught her how to apply for jobs with the CV and handwritten cover letter. After a few attempts, Adannaya got the hang of it. Every week, she would write applications and go to various office locations to submit them. Most of the companies were on the mainland Ikeja and Lagos Island area, and after taking the smaller Danfo buses for a while, she realised how expensive the transport fare was in Lagos and that her savings would run out if she did not make necessary adjustments.

Adannaya started to take the dreaded molue. It was uncomfortable initially, but she soon got used to the yelling bus conductors, the body odour emanating from the passengers around her, the hot and humid interior, and the constant struggle to get a seat on the bus. After waiting at bus stops for prolonged periods, the words "Mushin Olosha, Anthony Village, ma wole o!" sounded like music to her ears, and she looked forward to it because it meant she could get out of the hot sun and into the vehicle and proceed with her journey. Adannaya was gradually becoming a Lagos girl.

Job hunting wasn't all Adannaya did during that period. She also made time each week to visit her younger brother, Obioma, at Idumota on Lagos Island, where he was working as an apprentice to become a trader with Uncle Obiekwe's company.

Chief Obiekwe was a phenomenally successful millionaire businessman renowned for his amazing ability to mentor and train traders who became millionaires. Chief Obiekwe was credited with making about one hundred millionaires, both directly and indirectly. He was a great man.

Adannaya liked visiting the store to hang out with her brother and uncle. They were genuinely nice to her because they were proud of her achievements as a young female graduate. Adannaya carried out some administrative tasks for her uncle and acted as his personal secretary. She wrote letters, filed documents, and kept records. Uncle Obiekwe paid her an allowance for the work, and it couldn't have come at a better time because Adannaya was running out of funds as expected. Her savings would not last forever.

During her job search, Adannaya had to contend with men making passes at her when she dropped off her CV at some companies. They tried to take advantage of Adannaya and were quite blatant and direct about it.

"Beautiful girl, come and have dinner with me later, and the job is as good as yours,' they would say to her. As a Christian, Adannaya abhorred such practices and responded politely, "No, but thank you for the invitation." She was not the type to have an affair with a man to get a job. She knew she would get a job based on merit and not her looks, and she was prepared to wait and work hard no matter how long it took.

Adannaya did not have to wait too long. Three months after a persistent job search, she finally received an invitation to a job interview for the role of an advertising executive at a Crime Detective magazine. She was happy and relieved by the opportunity to be interviewed for employment because it was the closest she had come to getting a job in three months.

To prepare for the interview, Adannaya went to see Shade, who coached her thoroughly on what to wear and what to say at the interview. Adannaya was too excited to sleep the night before the interview. She ironed her best formal outfit, which was a navy blue skirt suit. She ironed it with spray starch to make the fabric firm and look more elegant. She polished her black court shoes until they shone.

That morning, Adannaya woke up very early, and she was careful not to disturb the other occupants of the bedroom. Since it was a full and rowdy house, she had to share a bedroom with her aunt's daughter. Adannaya dressed up carefully with minimal sound and left the house incredibly early because she knew Lagos traffic was unpredictable. She wanted to be punctual to create a good first impression.

Adannaya did not take the molue bus that day because she did not want to arrive sweaty and smelly from all the body odour emanating from the other passengers around her. She took the smaller danfo bus, which was cleaner, but the fare was more expensive. Adannaya did not want to arrive at her interview with dusty shoes, so she carried her shoes in a carrier bag to keep them clean. She put them on when she was a few metres away from the venue of the interview.

The interview was conducted by a panel of three men. There was no woman among them. The interview questions were similar to those Shade prepared and coached her on. Adannaya passed the interview and was offered the job immediately. The role of an Advertising Executive was to introduce the magazine to advertising agencies and solicit for them to recommend the magazine to their clients for their products and services to be advertised in the magazine. In a nutshell, the main remit of the job was to sell the ad spaces in the crime-fighting magazine. There was a basic pay and commission. Adannaya was elated.

Adannaya called her parents from the phone in Aunty Nkechi's house to tell them the good news and they were overjoyed. They could not believe she got a job in just three months. They were so proud of their exceptional daughter and shared the good news of her job with the extended family. Aunty Nkechi was happy that Adannaya finally got a job because she saw how much effort she put into the job search.

Adannaya was a quick learner and was able to kick-start the new job with ease. She was personable and had great interpersonal skills. These soft skills endeared her to the advertising agencies she had to deal with. She was able to meet her target of selling many ad spaces for the magazine.

Adannaya honoured that tradition and called to inform her father that she would send him her first salary. Chief Ugwumba, in his usual noble manner, advised her to give Aunty Nkechi the bulk of the salary that she would have sent to him and send him only a small amount. He also advised that Adannaya should pay her tithe (10% of earnings) in church, and the balance of the money should be retained for her travel expenses to work. Adannaya disbursed her salary just as her father advised. Aunty Nkechi prayed for her continued success. From her remaining money, Adannaya bought gifts and sent them to her three younger sisters. Her elder brother was already working in Warri. Her next salary was for Adannaya to spend however she wanted, and she did so.

Adannaya visited many advertising agencies to solicit for adverts. After an initial introduction to their media team, she would follow up with further visits until she received a decision on the ad placement. One of the agencies she frequented was Jade Marketing Communications Ltd, which was located in Anthony Village, Lagos. Unbeknownst to Adannaya, the media team at the agency had been discussing her. One day, the account manager of the media team stopped her for a chat. Adannaya thought she had done something wrong because she was only twenty-two years old and still new to the ways of the Lagos corporate world.

“Would you like to work in an advertising agency?”

The account manager’s question was unexpected, and she wondered why.

“What do you mean?”

“Will you consider a job in an advertising agency?” The account manager rephrased the question.

“Oh yes, it is something I would like to do. Why do you ask?”

“Because every time you come here, I notice how you relate with us and the passion with which you market your magazine to us.

“Thank you, sir,” grinned Adannaya.

“I told our CEO about you, and he said I should ask if you are interested in a career in advertising.”

“Yes, please. I am interested.”

The account manager liked her enthusiasm.

“Very good! You should apply for a job in our media department, and we will organise an interview for you.”

“Wow! Really?

“Yes, because we would like you to work for our company.”

“Thank you, sir,” said a grateful Adannaya. She was about to change her job without going through the rigour of making countless job applications. It was a dream come true.

Adannaya applied for the job and was hired. It was her entry into the world of advertising and the beginning of her advertising career. That was just three months after working at the Crime Detective magazine. There was a joke in their family that Adannaya changed jobs the way people change wrappers. Adannaya was a source of pride for her entire family from a noticeably early age, and she continued to do so in adulthood.

They were proud of her ability to achieve something that took other graduates years to accomplish.

Adannaya fell in love with the world of advertising and was eager to learn the end-to-end process of how things were done in advertising. She was exposed to the key departments in the advertising agency, from copyright to sales, media, account management, etc. The agency had a particularly good portfolio of high-profile clients like pharmaceutical companies, banks, etc. Adannaya loved her job and grew in her role within a year at the company.

A few months after starting her job at Jade Marketing Communication Ltd, Adannaya moved out of her auntie's house to live with her brother, Obioma. He had completed his apprenticeship with their uncle, who set him up with a few stores of his own. Since Obioma had spent a few years learning from the best, he became successful at business quite quickly, expanded the business with more stores, and had his own apprentices. Obioma rented a well-furnished house designed for maximum comfort. He decorated Adannaya's room beautifully and invited her to live with him. After almost a year of sharing a bedroom with her cousin in Aunty Nkechi's house, Adannaya was happy to have a room all to herself.

Shortly after Adannaya moved in with her brother, they received news that their father had had a stroke. The siblings decided that it would be better to bring their father to Lagos for treatment since the best hospitals were in Lagos. In addition, Obioma's house was big and comfortable enough for their father to live with them while he recovered from the stroke.

Adannaya travelled to NdiOrlu and brought her father to Lagos, and they settled him in the house. She had to wake up at 5 am during weekdays to prepare all her father needed before she left for work. She managed to juggle her job with caring for her dad. Obioma could see how Adannaya was struggling with maintaining her job and caring for their father simultaneously, and it involved frequent trips to the hospital. Adannaya could not take their father to the hospital without a car and often had to wait for Obioma to be available to take them to the hospital in his car.

Obioma had a surprise for Adannaya. One Saturday morning, he called her to the balcony of their top-floor flat and pointed at a sky-blue Toyota Carina parked in the driveway downstairs. He told her it was his gift to her and it would help with the running around she had to do as she juggled commuting to work and caring for their father.

Adannaya was speechless and hugged her brother with joy. She expressed her appreciation over and over again because she was so touched by his kindness. Adannaya had to learn how to drive quickly so she could start to make effective use of the car. She succeeded at that and discovered she enjoyed driving. She began driving to work and took her father to his hospital appointments. Life in Lagos became easier, and it was goodbye to the dreaded molue vehicles.

After a year at Jade Marketing Communications, Adannaya moved to another advertising agency. This time, it was CTWA, an international agency affiliated with an agency in the UK. Adannaya loved her job and wanted to continue in advertising. To achieve that, she needed to improve her skills and knowledge about advertising and obtain a professional qualification. Adannaya decided to go back to school and enroll for a postgraduate diploma in public relations and advertising at NIJ (Nigerian Institute of Journalism).

After her postgraduate diploma, Adannaya realised the only way she could become an accredited advertising practitioner was to obtain a diploma in Advertising from APCON (Advertising Practitioner Council of Nigeria). She enrolled for the course.

While Adannaya was studying at APCON, her boss suggested that she should enter the essay writing competition that APCON had advertised at the time. He knew Adannaya was a good writer and could win the competition. The topic was *The Development Of Advertising Profession in Nigeria.* Encouraged by her boss, Adannaya entered the competition.

To her amazement, Adannaya's essay was selected for second place price award by the Minister of Information at a grand occasion. The award was a cash prize and a plaque. That award was the highlight of Adannaya's advertising career, and it changed everything.

CHAPTER 4

The Job She Dreamed

The APCON essay award shot Adannaya into the limelight in the Nigerian advertising space. Adannaya was recognised as a trailblazer and confident advertising practitioner. APCON published the names of the winners in the daily newspapers because it was an inaugural award and the first of its kind. The news of the award circulated far and wide and to international audiences. Adannaya received a surprise congratulatory phone call from her cousin in Italy, who had read about the APCON Award and had seen her name on the list of winners in the newspapers.

Adannaya's church was immensely proud of the award as the news spread and celebrated it in the church in a typical Nigerian flamboyant thanksgiving party. Adannaya realised the award was a big deal considering all the attention it attracted to her. Unexpectedly, there was even more celebration to come.

Adannaya's employer, CTWA, had a party to celebrate her award in the office. As far as they were concerned, since one of their employees won the prestigious award, CTWA was also a winner.

CTWA invited advertising industry leaders to the party, who had wasted no time trying to poach the brilliant Adannaya. She was flattered and listened attentively to the various offers. Adannaya decided not to rush into accepting any of the job offers but to consider them carefully.

While Adannaya was contemplating which of the advertising job offers was the best for her, she read about a new international telecommunications company named GTTNet that had just been awarded a GSM (Global System for Mobile Communication) license in Nigeria. It was all over the daily newspapers, and GTTNet placed an ad vacancy for the role of customer service representatives and engineers.

It piqued Adannaya's interest because there was a buzz about this new company in Lagos. Everyone was excited about the fact that Nigerians would soon have GSM mobile phones and be able to communicate easily. Adannaya decided to learn more about it and asked a friend who worked at NIGTEL, the Nigerian national telecommunications company. Her friend confirmed everything Adannaya had heard about GTTNet and said it would change the world of communication in Nigeria forever. With that, Adannaya became certain that the telecommunications industry was the best move for her career progression. She carefully crafted her handwritten application, updated her CV, and submitted it for the role of Customer Service Representative.

Shortly after that, Adannaya dreamt her brother, Obioma, took her to Muritala Mohammed International Airport, Lagos, with her suitcases to board a flight abroad. Obioma was carrying Adannaya's suitcases as they walked into the airport together, and then Adannaya woke up.

"What a beautiful dream," mused Adannaya. She smiled at the thought of travelling abroad. She had never travelled abroad and wondered if it would ever happen. No one in Adannaya's immediate family had travelled abroad yet, and she knew it would be amazing if one of them did. Since Obioma was also in the dream, she wondered if the dream was about him going abroad on a business trip. Adannaya decided to tell him about the dream.

It was Saturday, and Obioma was having breakfast of boiled yam and scrambled eggs with a large cup of cocoa at the dining table. Obioma's favourite cocoa beverage was Milo chocolate drink; he always had it with his breakfast. Adannaya sat opposite him at the dining table.

"Obioma, you won't believe the dream I had last night."

"Dream? I hope it is not a bad dream!" He asked, frowning.

"What makes you think it is a bad dream?" Teased Adannaya

"Okay, since you are smiling, it must be a good dream then."

"Yes, it was. I dreamt you drove me to the airport to board a flight abroad." Adannaya described the entire dream to him.

Obioma laughed so much that he almost choked on his food. "Are you sure you don't have malaria? It is only malaria that can cause this type of dream!"

Adannaya couldn't help giggling at that. "No, be only malaria. Na typhoid sef."

"You better take a malaria tablet so you do not have such strange dreams anymore."

"It is not a strange dream o! You were even drinking your Milo in the dream sef!" Adannaya added to tease him.

"Me drinking milo in the dream? Mbanu! You know it is bad to eat in the dream, right?" Obioma shook his head in disagreement. No, I did not drink milo in your dream," he said emphatically.

Adannaya laughed at the horrified expression on her brother's face. "But why are you arguing about it? Is it your dream?" She teased again.

Obioma realised she was teasing him and burst into laughter as well. The siblings finally stopped laughing, and Adannaya headed for the kitchen to get breakfast. However, she could not resist another attempt to interpret her exciting dream.

"Maybe the dream is about you. I think you may be travelling abroad for business soon."

"No one is travelling abroad; it is just a 'malaria dream.' The malaria tablet is in the fridge o! Take two tablets quick, quick," advised Obioma as he returned to his breakfast.

Adannaya ignored her brother's advice. What is a 'malaria dream,' and who takes a 'malaria tablet' over a dream? It was ridiculous, and she knew that. She soon forgot about the dream and focused on eating her share of the boiled yam and scrambled eggs.

A week later, Adannaya received an invitation from GTTNet to participate in the recruitment process. The reputable international consultancy, Alexanders Consulting, managed the recruitment for the new roles. The consultancy was well known for its professionalism, and the applicants were not disappointed.

The Alexanders Consulting team were friendly and courteous to everyone. They patiently explained the recruitment process to the applicants. Most of them were foreigners, mostly British and Americans. There were over five hundred thousand applicants, and the consultants had the unenviable task of weeding through that substantial number of people to hire only forty customer service representatives and forty telecommunication engineers. Adannaya found out later that about five hundred thousand people applied for the eighty jobs. The unemployment problem in Nigeria was dire.

The recruitment process comprised three stages. First was the psychometric written test. Followed by the written competency-based test. The final stage was the oral interview. Adannaya was fascinated by the entire process. She had never done anything like that before, but she was happy to go through that process because it reminded her of her days in primary and secondary school, where she always beat her classmates to emerge top of the class. Although this was different, it was like another examination she had to pass. She rose to the challenge and worked hard at it. It was apparent that getting this job would be purely based on merit, nothing else. The best part was that the professional team did not flirt with the applicants, so Adannaya had no fear of anyone making passes at her this time.

The recruitment process took place at a venue with a large hall, and the applicants had to do it in batches. The Alexanders Consulting team were both male and female, and Adannaya was glad to see that women were heavily involved. She successfully completed the first and second stages of the recruitment process and observed that the total number of applicants had significantly decreased. She was pleased to still be among the remaining candidates.

At the final stage, Adannaya was invited to the oral interview, and she was glad to see a woman on the interview panel for a change. When she finished the recruitment process, she was satisfied with her performance because she knew she had given it her best shot. As faith was fundamental to Adannaya, she continued to pray daily for a positive outcome for this job interview.'

A few weeks later, Adannaya received a letter, which was delivered by a DHL courier. She took the parcel inside and sat in the living room to read it. When she opened the envelope, it was the GTTNet job offer. She almost fell off her seat after seeing the salary and benefits package. The amount was ten times higher than her current salary and beyond anything she had expected. “Wow!” She let out a whoop and danced around the room. Then she sat back down.

When Adannaya read the instructions about accepting the job offer, it included a line that she should send her Nigerian international passport along with the acceptance of the offer.

“What! My international passport? Wow! This is it! This was the dream I had. This is the job I dreamt of. I am travelling abroad!” Adannaya danced even longer this time, singing her favourite gospel song as she did so.

“What the Lord has done for me, I cannot tell it all.

What the Lord has done for me, I cannot tell it all.

What the Lord has done for me, I cannot tell it all,

He saved me and washed me in His blood.

So, I can shout Alleluia! I can shout Alleluia!

I can shout, praise the Lord.”

Adannaya rushed into her father’s room to tell him the wonderful news. He was still recovering from his stroke and was not back to his usual self yet. Adannaya wasn’t sure he understood what she told him, but he grinned broadly at her, so she believed he heard her clearly.

Obioma was blown away by the news when she told him. The siblings hugged and danced around the living room together.

"Do you remember that dream I told you about.? You said it was a 'malaria dream!'" Adannaya reminded him. She could not help gloating now.

"I know! I know!" Obioma conceded. "Don't mind me, biko."

"Who should go and take a malaria tablet now?" Teased Adannaya.

"Not you o! That dream was a revelation from God. It can only be God," admitted Obioma.

"Yes o! It can only be God," agreed Adannaya, and she started singing the gospel song again. Obioma joined her in singing and dancing as well.

Obioma was so proud of his elder sister and looked up to her. She was a high achiever and a major source of pride for their family. A role model and the best sister anyone could ever have. Obioma considered her a trail-blazer.

"You know the whole family is enormously proud of you already. Now they will be jumping up and down that one of us is finally going abroad."

"I know. I can't quite believe it yet. So, I will become the first person in our family to travel abroad." It suddenly dawned on Adannaya that she was about to accomplish something huge.

"Wait until Mama hears the news. She will make sure the whole of NdiOrlu hears about it."

"Oh Lord!" Adannaya exclaimed, cringing at the thought of her mum telling everyone about it.

Thankfully, Adannaya already had a Nigerian passport, so she sent it along with the acceptance of the job offer. Now, she could start preparing for her trip.

Adannaya travelled to NdiOrlu to break the exciting news to her mother and the rest of the family. Obioma was right about their mother's reaction to the news. When Adannaya told her, she ran outside their home and shouted loudly for her neighbours to hear that her daughter was travelling abroad to work. Adannaya tried to make her mother stop, but she did not listen.

"Mama, biko mechie ọnụ," Adannaya said repeatedly, but her mother's joy was great, and she could not help expressing it. Adannaya gave up and left her mum to it.

Adannaya understood the ways of the world to know that not everyone who congratulated her was happy with her good fortune. Some people were evil enough to be a hindrance to progress. So, Adannaya tried to stop her mother from spreading her daughter's good news, but she had to accept that she was under God's protection as a Christian and left it at that.

Her mum prayed for God's protection and blessings upon Adannaya as she embarked on her journey abroad. After a few days, Adannaya said goodbye to her mother and siblings and left for Lagos to prepare for her trip. She had resigned from CTWA and was in the last days of her notice period.

Days before her departure, Adannaya received her passport back from her new employer, and it came with a visa to South Africa and Zimbabwe.

Alexanders Consulting were also in charge of the onboarding process, which involved induction and training in Zimbabwe. All the successful candidates (forty of them) were told the time to arrive at the airport, and where to meet so they could have dinner together before departure. They were to be briefed on the itinerary, the training, and the duration of the training period.

Obioma drove Adannaya to the airport with her suitcases. He helped her to carry them into the airport and waved goodbye at her. It was exactly how it happened in her dream. Adannaya could not help reminding him of the dream once more, and they both laughed at the memory of his insistence that it was a 'malaria dream'".

Adannaya joined the other new employees in the waiting area. Everything went as planned, and they were soon on board the flight to South Africa. Their destination was Zimbabwe, but they had to take a transit flight with a one-night stopover in South Africa. Their employer, GTTNet, seized the opportunity to show the new employees the company headquarters in South Africa. The launch of GTTNet GSM services in Nigeria was a big achievement for the company because they beat other companies to emerge as the first company to win the bid for the GSM licence in Nigeria. The new employees were welcomed by the GTTNet Managing Director, who was incredibly happy to meet the Nigerian team.

The next day, they boarded the connecting flight to Zimbabwe, which became Adannaya's residence for the next three months, where she underwent induction and training. Their accommodation was a delightful hotel.

The customer service representatives went to work in the head office and were trained to work in the call centre and GTTNet Stores. They used the buddy system to pair each Customer Service Representative with an experienced CS rep in Zimbabwe. The new engineers were also paired up with the experienced engineers on the site where they worked in Zimbabwe. They all worked side-by-side.

It wasn't all work because the new employees had a lot of fun, too. They travelled to neighbouring countries like Botswana for sightseeing, and Adannaya had the opportunity to buy lovely gifts for her family. There were also dinner parties, and the most remarkable one was the one at the Nigerian High Commission. It was hosted by the High Commissioner, and the Nigerian team were treated to some delicious Nigerian delicacies.

One thing Adannaya loved most about her new job was the fact that her employers were devoted Pentecostal Christians. They also practised their faith at work, which was why every workday started with a morning devotion in which all the employees gathered together for prayers. Due to Adannaya's Christian devotion, she quickly stood out among the Nigerian team of new employees. She led a few of the prayer sessions, and this drew the attention of the managing director, and he came to notice Adannaya, a CS Rep. He took an interest in her and introduced her to a community of professional Christians known as APOSTLES IN THE MARKETPLACE.

At the end of the training, Adannaya and the rest of the new employees returned to Nigeria. Adannaya gave her family the beautiful gifts she bought for them, and her mother loved the ivory jewellery from Botswana so much that she would not stop wearing it for months.

GTTNet finally launched the GSM network in Nigeria, and the new team took their place at the call centre. The GTTNet stores were not yet built at the time, so all the CS Reps had to work at the call centre. Adannaya was one of the first group of people to own a mobile phone in the country, and the day she took it home, many people came to Adannaya to see what a mobile phone looked like. Adannaya continued to attend the prayer sessions with 'The Apostles of the Marketplace.'

Adannaya excelled at her job once again, and after six months, she was made a Call Centre supervisor. Her line manager was an expatriate, a white South African. When he went away on annual leave, Adannaya stood in for him and carried on with the responsibility of managing the operations of the Call centre.

When it became apparent that the South African call centre manager was not going to return to his position, the company decided to find someone within the company to replace him instead of hiring another expatriate for the job. The general manager discussed it with the Managing Director and recommended Adannaya for the job. He believed she had the right aptitude and would be great at the job once she received the necessary training. The Managing Director knew who Adannaya was and had heard good things about her performance, so they approved without hesitation.

When the general manager broke the news to Adannaya, she almost fainted in shock because it was totally unexpected. She expressed her concern that she might not be well equipped for the role, but the general manager brushed that aside and promised to give her all the support she needed. He was an engineer. He also reminded Adannaya that she was already doing an excellent job of standing in for the call centre manager position; therefore, she might as well accept the role and get paid for it.

Adannaya was glad to learn that the company recognised her hard work and performance and that she was being rewarded for it. She accepted the new role as the Call centre manager, which came with a bigger Remuneration. The proverbial 'icing on the cake' was that Adannaya received three months' salary arrears for the period her manager was away, and she functioned in an acting capacity.

It was a reasonable sum of money, and when the HR manager saw the amount on the payroll, he called Adannaya and advised her to make effective use of the funds. He asked Adannaya to visit his family home during the weekend, and he would recommend some investment options to her. Adannaya appreciated the fact that the HR manager cared enough to do that, and she did not hesitate to visit him as he suggested. His investment advice was to buy a piece of land in the affluent Lekki area of Lagos.

Adannaya could see it was a brilliant idea, and she bought the land with the help of the HR manager, who was kind enough to guide her through the process and completion of the transaction. Adannaya was a trailblazer once again, as it was rare for a young woman to make such an investment at that time.

An incident occurred that tested Adannaya's leadership skills. One day, one of Adannaya's CS Reps collapsed at work. She had him taken to the hospital reserved for expatriates because of the quality of care they gave, but it was the nearest hospital to the office. The CS Rep received immediate and high-quality medical treatment, and he recovered.

When the hospital bill was sent to the office, the HR department was not happy about it, and they queried Adannaya for taking the CS Rep to the expensive hospital reserved for expatriates instead of the local hospital for Nigerian employees. Adannaya was unhappy about the query and decided to escalate the matter to her boss, the general manager. She marched into his office and spoke her mind.

"Oga, please tell those HR people that the blood that flows in this young man's veins is the same blood that flows in the veins of the expatriates. You know I have the highest number of staff in this building. I have 112 out of the total staff of 180 and they run three shifts. If they push this matter one more time, I will tell my people exactly what happened, and we shall organise a demonstration in front of this building tomorrow. This company surely does not need that headline in the newspapers tomorrow!

The general manager knew Adannaya was upset, so he tried calming her down.

"*Abeg Adannaya, you no say you stubborn well well. I no wan wahala I beg.* Wait, let me go and settle the matter."

The general manager reprimanded the HR team and told them to back off. They listened to him and closed the case. Based on that episode, Adannaya was jokingly nicknamed the highest union leader in the office.

Everything was running smoothly for Adannaya and her team. She organised team-away days for them. She was a good manager, efficient, supportive, and empathetic. She often dropped by the office on Sundays to check on her team. They knew they could talk to her about anything bothering them, and she would support them to the best of her abilities.

That year, Adannaya was presented with an award for the best team manager at GTTNet. The Chairman of GTTNet came from Zimbabwe to present the award to her in person because executive management recognised that running a successful call centre was not an easy feat to achieve. That award further raised Adannaya's profile in the company.

As a call centre manager, Adannaya was responsible for approving visa application letters for her team of CS Reps who wanted to travel abroad on holiday. The visa applications were successful, and Adannaya saw many of her team members enjoying trips abroad to the UK and USA. She decided to apply for those visas, including the Schengen visa, and they were all issued to her.

A sad event occurred during this period. The amazing and lovable Chief Ugwumba passed on. He never recovered from the stroke that left him bedridden and eventually took his life. Adannaya was devastated, and it was a very painful loss for their family. She was achieving many remarkable things, and her beloved father was no longer alive to witness it, and that made his death unbearable for Adannaya. She felt her world had collapsed because her father was her rock. She took comfort in the fact that she was living with her brother, Obioma, and her younger sister, Nwanneka. As siblings, they could share in the grief together. It would have been worse if she lived alone.

GTTNet was growing bigger and expanding into different states. A marketing department was created, and the roles of media manager and event manager were advertised. Adannaya saw this as an opportunity to return to doing what she loved. Media and advertising were her career roots. Adannaya applied for the media manager job and was successful.

Her boss, the general manager, was reluctant to let her go and fought with the marketing director over Adannaya, but the director insisted on having Adannaya on his team, and since it was what she wanted, her boss had to give in.

Adannaya easily blossomed in that role because the media manager oversaw public relations and advertising, an industry that Adannaya knew very well. She also had post graduate qualifications in both fields; therefore, it was a no-brainer that this was a perfect fit for her next career move. Adannaya had all her old contacts in the industry, and she reconnected with them to get the job done. She eased into the role like it was tailor-made for her.

One of the perks of the new role was an official car and driver. It was a brand-new Toyota Avensis car. Adannaya was managing a budget of about two hundred million naira every six months, which grew to a budget of about two billion naira as GTTNet continued to expand all over Nigeria. There was GTTNet Ibadan, GTTNet NdiOrlu, and so on.

The company decided that the media department had become too big and had to be restructured. The department was upgraded to a division, and Adannaya was promoted to head of the media division. This drastically changed Adannaya's remuneration. She was earning a fantastic salary, and her official car was a brand-new BMW, which was later replaced with a brand-new PRADO Jeep and a driver.

Once again, Adannaya had broken the proverbial 'glass ceiling' with her achievements. She was a trailblazer in her career because of all the awards she had won and her rapid career progression. Adannaya was also a trailblazer in her family because of her top job and owning a property in a choice part of a metropolitan city like Lagos.

Adannaya was in a wonderfully comfortable position in her career, and she decided this was the perfect time to embark on her first holiday abroad. She had been working incredibly hard to develop her career while coping with the loss of her beloved father. Therefore, a nice break from work and Nigeria was long overdue. She needed a change of scene to go out and see the world.

Adannaya had all the visas she needed. Where should she go? She was spoilt for choice. And the world, as it were, was her oyster.

CHAPTER

5

A Lasting Holiday Romance

Adannaya's first holiday abroad was to London, United Kingdom. Adannaya stayed with a relative- Uncle Tom, who picked her up from Heathrow airport and showed her how to get around the city using the trains and buses. Adannaya was fascinated by the underground trains that Londoners called the Tube. There were many of them differentiated by their colours. For example, the red line was the Circle line, the black one was the Northern line, etc. It was a very quick mode of travel, and there was a map to help you navigate your journey around London. To a tourist, this was quite convenient, and Adannaya loved taking the tube. She visited Buckingham Palace, Madame Tussaud, and other popular tourist attractions in the city.

Adannaya experienced a culture shock based on what she observed about the UK. She saw people queuing in an orderly manner to get on the bus, trains, and everywhere. This never happened in rowdy Lagos. It was always a rush to do anything, which could best be described jokingly as 'the survival of the fittest.'

Adannaya observed the cultural differences in the way people in the UK spoke to each other. They were quite formal and indirect in their manner of speech and approach compared to the Nigerian approach, which was more direct. Adannaya realised quickly when shopping that you cannot haggle over prices like in Nigeria. You have to pay whatever price was displayed on the item. Adannaya did all her shopping with cash; they were mostly substantial since she bought shoes and clothing to sell back home in Lagos. She was surprised to receive curious glances from the sellers as she paid with higher denominations. She later learned that people usually pay higher amounts with cards in the UK, unlike Lagos, which was predominantly a cash economy.

Adannaya also visited her immediate younger sister -Chioma, in New York, USA. After visiting the UK and the USA, Adannaya decided her next holiday destination would be Italy, where she had many relatives. She had a Schengen visa and decided to travel through France to see the Eiffel Towers in Paris. Adannaya arrived in Venice, where she was warmly welcomed by her dear cousin Chinyere, with whom she stayed throughout her holiday. Venice was a seaside town full of canals, and people travelled around the town in gondolas. Adannaya had never seen anything like it and found it fascinating.

Venice was a romantic city; what better place to have a holiday romance than Venice. It was a beautiful city built on islands in a lagoon with many canals and bridges and few roads. Couples loved to ride and cuddle in gondolas with beautiful music playing in the background. Adannaya loved the food because Italians cooked great food, and she ate lots of pasta and spaghetti. Every meal was special and beautifully made. She also noticed that the Italians prioritised their quality of life over everything else, which explained why they took lunch breaks from work in the afternoon to go home to rest. It was a huge cultural shock, and Adannaya could not imagine that happening in Nigeria, where earning an income from a job or business was considered the priority over anything else.

Adannaya struggled with the language barrier because nearly everyone spoke Italian, and all the road signs were also in Italian. Luckily for her, she had her cousin Chinyere and other relatives with her when she went out, and they helped with the communication barrier.

One day, Adannaya attended an Igbo community meeting popularly known in the Diaspora as a 'Village meeting.' She met her secondary school classmate and family friend Ngozi. They were such close friends that they used to spend the night in each other's homes, and their brothers were good friends too. They were so happy to reconnect again.

At the event, Ngozi introduced Adannaya to her cousin, Chima, and they hit it off and became friends. The friendship blossomed into a holiday romance, and Adannaya got quite close to Chima during her three weeks holiday in Italy. Although Adannaya was reluctant to start a relationship, knowing she was only going to be in Italy for three weeks, the mutual attraction was irresistible, and they fell in love.

Chima Mbadiwe was a very handsome man, tall with a chocolate brown complexion and a gorgeous physique. He had the kind of personality Adannaya was usually attracted to because it complemented her personality, which was on the serious side. Chima worked in a factory and was often away at work during the day.

Adannaya focused on shopping for goods to sell as usual. Chima did not only show her where to shop, but he also went with her. They travelled to Napoli together to buy leather shoes, belts, and bags because Italy was known for her top-quality leather products. Since

Adannaya did not speak Italian, she was glad that Chima accompanied her on her shopping trips to help with the communication barrier.

After Adannaya returned to Nigeria, the romance with Chima continued, and it became a long-distance relationship instead of just a holiday romance. Thank God for mobile phones because the lovebirds were able to stay in contact on the phone. They had several long conversations and got to know each other even better.

Ngozi and her brothers were happy that Adannaya was dating their cousin, Chima, and they pressured her to marry him. The families were from neighbouring towns and knew each other well. Chima's family was happy he was dating Adannaya because they knew she was from a good family. They were family friends, after all. Nonetheless, Adannaya was surprised at how much pressure the family put on her to marry Chima.

Adannaya knew she had not dated Chima for long or knew him well enough, but she loved him and believed that his family considered them a good match. When Chima proposed, she accepted his proposal, and they started to make plans for their future together.

The couple agreed that Chima would move back to Nigeria since Adannaya had an exceptionally decent job as head of Media at GTTNet. Adannaya would not relocate to Italy. Their entire plan would require an entire year to execute, which would give Chima the required time to sort out his affairs and round off everything in Italy so that he could move to Nigeria permanently.

In addition, they would follow the Nigerian tradition and have the usual three marriage ceremonies: the traditional marriage in NdiOrlu, the church wedding in Italy and the registry marriage in Lagos. It was going to be a combination of local and exotic marriage ceremonies.

Chima did not have to travel to Nigeria to participate in the traditional marriage. This was not unusual in the Igbo culture. Their parents and extended families organised the ceremony on behalf of the couple and got a male relative to stand in for Chima. Adannaya returned to the village a week before the date to help with the planning. Adannaya's Uncle Mazi explained that the date for the traditional marriage was selected based on the Igbo four-market days. So, the traditional market day selected was Eke day. Prior to Adannaya's arrival, her proud mum and relatives decorated the compound and invited the extended family relatives and kindred. As often happens in villages, the news of the traditional marriage ceremony spread and a lot of people from the village turned up on the day of the event. They were excited to see Adannaya, whom many of them had last seen during her secondary school days.

As soon as the date was agreed, Chima's family collected the list of requirements for the traditional marriage. This includes:

1. 1 big goat
2. 8 kegs of Palm Wine
3. George wrappers
4. 8 tubers of yam
5. 4 cartons of malt drinks
6. 8 cartons of beer
7. 2 bottles of original Seaman's schnapps
8. 8 kolanuts
9. 8 alligator pepper
10. 4 heads of tobacco
11. 1 bottle of ground tobacco snuff
12. 4 heads of Igbo wrappers
13. 2 kegs of upwine

Adannaya dressed in traditional Igbo bridal attire of embroidered skirt and blouse, topped with complimentary beads on her beautiful, plaited hair. She wore a special ivory necklace and bracelet from her grandmother's collection. The elders were gathered at her father's Obi (square). Adannaya 's mother reminded her to go and great them before Chima's family arrived. The elders were pleased with Adannaya when she came out to greet them and commented on how beautiful she looked.

By 10 am, the chairs under the canopies were fully occupied by the relatives and village members. The men were preparing the cow and goat meat while the women were cooking jollof rice, stew, bitter leaf, and egusi soup. The young men helped to pound the yam.

The festive atmosphere was ignited even more when Chima's family arrived with traditional dancers, and they performed to everyone's delight. Everyone joined in the song and dance for the bride and groom.

Everyone was gathered in Adannaya's father's house. There were canopies where most of the guests and family members sat. There was also an outhouse known as the 'Obi' where the male family members and representatives from both sides gathered to conduct the traditional marriage. As was the tradition, when the men concluded their deliberations, they would join the rest of the guests under the canopy to celebrate the occasion.

After the traditional breaking of the kolanut to welcome the visitors, the appointed witness to the marriage was someone who knew both families and acted as a mediator for both sides. He also facilitated the ceremony, and the name of the witness on this occasion was Chief Okeke.

Chief Okeke stood up in the Obi to start the traditional marriage ceremony. "Welcome, my people. Many of you have travelled far and near to this happy occasion, so I welcome you all," He greeted them.

There were murmurs of "Thank you. Thank you."

"We have the family of the bride and groom here today. The Mbadiwe family and Ugwumba family. You are all welcome."

"Who is representing the Mbadiwe family?" He asked as he sat down.

The respective families are usually represented by the fathers of the couple getting married, but since both Adannaya's father and Chima's father passed away, they were represented by other family members. For Chima, it was his elder brother, Chief Chinedu. Adannaya's family was represented by her uncle, Chief Mazi. The introductions were done.

Adannaya, the bride, was not required at the ceremony at this point and was inside the main house, getting dressed and waiting to be called in.

Chief Okeke called the representative of the groom's family to speak first. "We ask the Mbadiwe family to tell us why they are here."

Chief Chinedu stood up to speak. "There is this beautiful flower we found, and we are very interested in plucking this flower, but we know that someone in this family nurtured the flower so we have come to seek permission to pluck it and take it home."

There was general laughter and giggling from the audience. Chief Chinedu also laughed because he knew he was in for a gentle grilling, but it was all in humour.

Adannaya's elders in the Obi mumbled, "We don't know what you're talking about," and they laughed.

Some of them said, "We don't know which flower because we have so many beautiful flowers that are growing in this compound. We don't know which one you are talking about."

Chief Okeke asked Chief Chinedu to clarify.

"Are you sure? Are you sure this is the place that the flower is growing?"

Chief Chinedu was expecting it. "Yes, this is the place. The flower is growing in the Ugwumba's compound here."

The next question came from Adannaya's family. "So, who saw this flower?"

Chief Chinedu responded as his father would if he were there. "My son saw the flower."

Adannaya's relatives began to whisper among themselves (as they do in the village), pretending to guess who the bride was.

"Okay, no problem. Do you know the name of this flower?" Chief Okeke asked.

"Yes, we know the name. She is called Adannaya Ugwumba." answered Chief Chinedu.

Chief Okeke then addressed Adannaya's uncle Mazi. "Do you have any flower by that name in this house?"

Uncle Mazi answered straight away. "Yes, we do."

"Good. Can we see the flower?"

Adannaya's aunties were waiting under the canopy and ready for that moment in the ceremony. As soon as they received the signal, they quickly informed Adannaya, who was still inside the main house with her bridesmaids.

Adannaya was escorted by a few of her bridesmaids, who danced into the Obi with Adannaya behind them as the last person to enter. She was dressed in the most beautiful Igbo native attire in the chosen colour scheme for the traditional marriage, olive green and gold colours with beads around her waist, ankles, and wrists. Her friends departed, and Adannaya stopped in the middle of the Obi and waited for Chief Okeke to continue. Adannaya's mother had explained the order of the ceremony to her, so she knew what to do.

Everyone remarked on how gorgeous she looked; it was a beautiful flower to behold. There were murmurs of "ah" and "Ehe." Some said, "chai, but you people know how to choose a good wife o!" Adannaya tried not to laugh, but she could not help but smile at their words.

Chief Okeke grinned and continued. He turned to Chief Chinedu and said, "Is this the flower you are looking for?"

"Yes, yes! This is the one," and everyone clapped joyously.

"Our wife, come and sit with us," beckoned members of Chima's family.

"No, no, no, Mba! It is not time for that yet. She is not your wife yet," said Chief Okeke

"Look for the person who proposed to you and give him this glass of palm wine." They handed Adannaya the drink.

As she made her way towards Chima's relatives, the younger men shouted, "Give me! Give me! It is me! This way! Give me the palm wine."

Adannaya grinned as she tried to find Chief Chinedu, whom she knew was standing in for her fiancé, Chima. Then, as she walked towards him and knelt in front of him to give him the palm wine, there was a lot of clapping and whooping!

Chief Chinedu accepted the glass from her and drank the wine. "Thank you he said as he took her hand, pulled her to her feet, and asked her to sit beside him. Everybody was happy because it was a sign that Adannaya had accepted the marriage proposal. Chief Okeke invited the elders to pray for Adannaya and Chima. They prayed and blessed them for good health and prosperity and lots of children, male and female.

Following this, they asked Adannaya to return to the main house while the remaining part of the ceremony continued. As Adannaya walked out of the Obi with smiles through the canopy area to the main house, there were cheers from the Obi and the guests in the canopy area. Everyone knew that the deal was sealed. The guests in the canopy rushed to accompany her to the main house, congratulating and commending her attire and how beautiful she looked.

As required by tradition, the men in the Obi moved on to the next phase of the marriage procedure, which was the '*Ima ogu aku*' or bride price negotiation in English. As the discussion was taking place in the Obi by the elders, they began to whisper so they could not be overheard.

Chief Okeke handed over to the elders from both families and invited them to proceed. Uncle Mazi gave a bunch of native brooms (a big bunch of tiny broomsticks tied with a string) to Chief Chijioke, Chima's eldest relative in the meeting.

"Take this broom and remove any quantity your family would like," he said.

Chief Chijioke took the broom, put his hand in it, took out some quantity of the broomsticks, and gave Uncle Mazi what was left of the broom.

"Now count the number of the broomsticks and multiply by whatever number your family would like to," Uncle Mazi said.

Chief Chijioke and his family whispered together and agreed on a denomination, and they multiplied the broomsticks by that number to determine the bride price. It was all done discreetly as the tradition dictated. After both parties had agreed, Chief Chijioke immediately handed the amount to Uncle Mazi. Following this, Chief Okeke announced that the bride's price had been agreed upon. Everyone clapped and exchanged handshakes across both families. Now that the brideprice had been paid and accepted, Chief Chinedu and his family brought out all the other items that Adannaya's family had requested from them. They laid it all out for everyone to see.

Uncle Mazi stood up, thanked the Mbadiwe family for their gifts, and accepted them on behalf of the Ugwumba family. The two families hugged each other with lots of handshakes and traditional name greetings. They prayed for and blessed the couple one more time. Adannaya and Chima were now married in the Igbo tradition, and it was time to celebrate. Chief Okeke concluded the conversations and asked everyone to move over to the canopies for the celebration. Everyone was happy as they enjoyed the delicious food and drinks. The DJ played great music. Adannaya's bridesmaids escorted her to the dancing floor. Everyone danced to their heart's content. The music and entertainment went on throughout until evening and the end of the ceremony. After the traditional marriage, the two families agreed that the church wedding would go ahead in Italy and that the court marriage would be held in Lagos, Nigeria.

Adannaya and Chima were excited about the Church wedding scheduled to take place in Venice, Italy. The couple knew they had many friends and relatives to support them and make the ceremony happy and memorable. Getting married in Italy was exactly what Adannaya needed to have the small wedding of her dreams. Her high profile was a guarantee that it would attract a large crowd, which she did not want and was keen to avoid.

The special day arrived, and Adannaya's cousin -Dike, walked her down the aisle. It was a beautiful ceremony, and Adannaya wore the most spectacular white couture wedding gown from one of the best fashion designers in Italy. Chima was gorgeous in his dark grey tuxedo. They were a dream couple. After the wedding, Adannaya stayed back in Italy for the honeymoon with her new husband. The newlyweds had a wonderful two weeks together before Adannaya left to visit her younger sister Chioma in the USA. She returned to Nigeria shortly after that.

Back in Lagos, Adannaya received many wedding presents from her work colleagues, friends, and family, who were so happy for her. Adannaya's euphoria lasted for a long time because she had married the man she loved and had a beautiful wedding. She was now looking forward to married life and having babies with Chima.

She had to wait for many months before she could live with her husband, but at least she was not living alone. Adannaya continued to live with her brothers, Obioma and Nwanneka. Chima arrived in Nigeria a year later and was welcomed warmly by his wife, Adannaya. They had their registry marriage, and this time, it was a quiet ceremony with a few guests to witness it. They moved into their beautiful new house in Lekki, Victoria Island, and started married life.

Adannaya was already involved in running a few businesses she owned and doing her job at GTTNet. The couple agreed that Adannaya would hand the businesses over to Chima for management. There was a telecom dealership company, a popular Bar and restaurant, transportation, and a grocery store. Chima happily took over the management of the business chain, and Adannaya focused on her high-profile job.

The dynamics of their relationship - a highly accomplished woman and a high-flyer who was quite successful was married to a typical African man who had yet to establish financial independence as his wife began to strain their relationship. Chima did not like having to live under her shadow.

The couple's plan was to start a family as soon as possible, but it was delayed due to initial fertility challenges. Culturally, wives are perceived as having difficulties when a couple struggles to conceive. Thankfully, the fertility challenges the couple had could be treated, and so they commenced the treatment.

Soon, Chima became frustrated by the challenges they were facing in the marriage, making him irritable and lashing out at Adannaya. He was short-tempered and threw harmful objects at her, including bottles, lamps, and even hot soup from the cooking pot. This marked the beginning of the domestic abuse Adannaya endured for months and years, which also included financial and emotional abuse.

Chima began to cheat on Adannaya with a string of affairs with various women. His infidelity bothered her, but as a Christian, she was focused on prayers. His abusive behaviour towards her was scarier. Chima tried to hide his affairs from Adannaya, but some of them were so blatant and 'close to home' that it was inevitable that she would find out about them, and she did.

Surprisingly, it was revealed that Chima had impregnated a female domestic staff at their restaurant. The shock wasn't just the obvious embarrassment of having a relationship with a domestic staff; it was also because Chima impregnated a teenager. Chima denied it, of course, and said it was all a lie. He dismissed the staff.

Adannaya could not wrap her head around it. What kind of man did she marry, she wondered over and over again. He was like a stranger and someone she barely knew. She complained to her friend and Chima's cousin, Ngozi. Adannaya was shocked that Ngozi blamed the girl rather than Chima, who abused a vulnerable girl.

The situation was sickening, and Adannaya found it unbearable. She became depressed and a shadow of her former self. It was a very messy situation, and Adannaya tried desperately to keep away from the media. She was always in the news professionally as the head of media, launching one product or the other for GTTNet. Her high profile would make this news a scandalous story. This filled Adannaya with anxiety and fear for her reputation. Thankfully, she succeeded in the end, and the scandal never became public, but it took its toll on her as more of Chima's affairs were revealed to her.

Adannaya could not get over what had happened, and remaining in that house with her abusive husband, Chima, only made her feel worse. Adannaya decided to go and stay with her siblings Obioma and Nwanneka for a while. However, it did not make any difference because Adannaya was deeply hurt, and the air of melancholy around was obvious for all to see. She lost her appetite and ate little, which resulted in weight loss. She had bags under her eyes due to countless sleepless nights. Adannaya just wanted to be left alone and did not want to talk about her miserable marriage.

Obioma became overly concerned about her and informed their elder brother, Akachi, in Port Harcourt, and he came rushing down to Lagos for the weekend. Both brothers tried to find out what was wrong with Adannaya. They were not sure if she was ill or just depressed.

The brothers were standing in Adannaya's bedroom, watching her on the bed where she lay with the covers over her head as if to shut out the entire world. Like most people wallowing in depression, she wanted to hide from the world and never got out of bed unless when necessary. Thankfully, Obioma knew exactly what was happening and told Akachi about it.

"I know what is wrong with her."

"Really? What is it? What is it?" Asked a worried Akachi.

"It is Chima! That is the name of her illness. That man will be the death of her," answered Obioma.

"How can you say he will be the death of her? What happened? Pressed Akachi

Obioma recounted everything Adannaya had told him about the difficult situation in her marriage, with emphasis on abusive behaviour and infidelity.

"This is terrible! How long has this been going on? Asked a horrified Akachi. Why am I just hearing this now?

"It is because I did not know it was this bad. Do you know that two months after Chima came and Adannaya moved in with him, she told me that the marriage would not work, but I did not believe her, and I told her that it was too early to draw that conclusion," explained Obioma.

"How can you dismiss what she said just like that? Were you living under the same roof with them? Scolded their big brother, Akachi.

"Well, I was only trying to encourage her to work on her marriage. After all, it was only after two months," said Obioma defensively.

"I know, but..." Akachi was interrupted by Obioma.

"Would you have allowed her to give up on her marriage so soon?"

"Hmmm.... I don't know, but it is not that simple," added Akachi.

Adannaya was fed up with hearing them talk about her as though she was not there. She pulled down the blanket over her face and sat up. She knew she had to say something; otherwise, they would not leave her alone.

"I cannot give up on my marriage yet because I want God to bless me with a child."

Her elder brother was glad to finally have a conversation with her, and he sat beside her on the bed. Obioma remained standing.

"I understand that, but how will you bring a child into this toxic situation?" Akachi asked.

"Sis, it is better that you are alive and away from this man than for you to die and be married!" Warned Obioma.

"Obi, how can you say it like that? Don't mention the word dead or death again. This is the second time," Akachi said, reprimanding Obioma once again. He knew Obioma was right, but Akachi did not want Adannaya to hear such things in her condition because she would feel even worse than she did already.

Adannaya shook her head. “No, he cannot kill me, not when he is benefiting so much from the marriage.”

“Hmmm…that is true, but is that not a reason for him to even treat you better?” Akachi asked.

“That is the more reason why he is treating her so badly,” Obioma said.

“Yes, we know the type. He is intimidated by his wife’s high profile, and he is small-minded enough to think that treating her this way would put her in her place and make her fear him,” Akachi concluded.

“Exactly! That is what he is doing. Chima does not know how lucky he is. He should be grateful to his wife and appreciate her more,” agreed Obioma.

“Only decent men reason like that; my brother and Chima are obviously not good men,” added Akachi.

“Can’t we just go and beat him up to teach him a lesson? In fact, let me go and plan with our in-law, Ogechi’s, husband to arrange to teach him some lessons!” Sugested an increasingly angry Obioma.

Akachi did not like that. “That is not who we are in this family. We do not behave like that. Papa will be turning in his grave hearing those words.”

Adannaya felt like diving under her blanket once more. They were talking about her once again as though she was not there.

"Besides, we are family friends with Chima's family," argued Akachi.

"Yes, you were one of the people who encouraged me to marry Chima because he is your friend's cousin," said Adannaya.

"That is true, Akachi. Why did you encourage Adannaya to marry this terrible man?" Like any younger brother, Obioma was tired of being reprimanded by his elder brother and seized the opportunity to let him know that he also messed up, but in a respectful manner, of course.

"Both of you are talking as if I knew Chima was a bad person when I encouraged my own sister to marry him." Said Akachi defensively.

Adannaya knew that and reassured him. "Of course, you did not know that. Maybe it is my fault for not getting to know him better," she said, close to tears.

"No, no, I am your elder brother, and I should have found out all I could about Chima instead of believing what Emeka told me," admitted Akachi.

"That is true," nodded Obioma. "So, what do we do about the situation now?"

"It is time to talk to Chima's family about how we are not happy with what is going on. I will start with his cousins because they are close to him."

"That is a good idea," agreed Obioma. "What do you think, Sis?"

"Well... maybe it would help. I think it is worth a try." Adannaya knew it wouldn't make any difference because Chima's family, especially his cousins, knew exactly who he was before they encouraged Adannaya to marry him. But she did not say that. Otherwise, Akachi would give up on the idea. Adannaya was curious to see if taking that step would help save her marriage in any way.

Akachi decided to change the topic and move Adannaya's mind away from the sad situation. "How are you coping at work with all these?"

"I called in sick because I do not feel well anyway."

"Maybe you should take a holiday and go to America to clear your head. I am sure Chioma will be happy to have you over for a while," suggested Akachi. This was something he had agreed with Obioma that they should encourage Adannaya to do.

"Yes, Adannaya is always in a happier mood when she returns from America." Obioma added, and the brothers laughed. Adannaya managed a smile.

Adannaya had already considered that but wasn't sure she was in the right frame of mind for a trip abroad. Then she realised that getting far away from Nigeria at that moment might do the trick.

"Oh, okay. I will speak to my boss on Monday and request for some annual leave.

"Fantastic!" Smiled Akachi. We will buy you the flight ticket as a gift from Obioma and I."

"But you don't have to do that. You have your family responsibility." Adannaya did not want to bother them like that.

Akachi raised his hand up to interrupt her. "It is not up for debate. We have settled it."

"Yes, we have o! Biko let us go and eat. I am starving. They have prepared fufu and bitter leaf soup for us," said Obioma, who brought the discussion to a successful conclusion. The three siblings left the room together.

While Adannaya was away in the USA, she contemplated what her next step should be. She desperately wanted to have a child and believed that it would happen if she stayed in her marriage, especially now that her husband successfully impregnated someone.

As a devout Christian, would divorce be an option? How could she tell her pastors and church members that she wanted to divorce the husband she chose herself and a man unknown to the church? They would simply tell her that "divorce was not of God and that God hates divorce." Besides, what would she do after the divorce?

Date different men to get pregnant or find another husband? She recoiled just thinking about it.

When Adannaya returned to Nigeria, her faith in God kept her going. She believed her fervent prayers would save her marriage. In the name of Jesus, her husband would change and become a good man. Adannaya only had to pray harder for it to happen. That was her conviction, and she fasted for days. She travelled to the well-known prayer mountain on the outskirts of Lagos to pray about her marriage.

The prayer mountain was regarded as a sacred location where people, especially those of Pentecostal and evangelical faith, sought solitude and support from other prayer warriors for divine intervention regarding difficult life challenges. The mountain was located in a remote village surrounded by shrubs and trees that were regularly maintained by a vibrant rural Pentecostal church within the precinct. Their work was funded through offerings and donations by the pilgrims who came to seek spiritual succour. The mountain had four levels with steep stones as steps for worshippers to climb. On the day Adannaya arrived at the site, she met a lot of people at the lower level of the mountain, with some on the second and third levels. When Adannaya looked up, she noticed a few people on the fourth and last level receiving prayers from some prayer warriors. In her characteristic determination, Adannaya climbed to the highest point of the mountain, where she met the prayer leader, known as the prophet. He prayed for Adannaya and decreed that God would answer her prayers and bless her with a child, and the future would be bright for her and her family. He advised Adannaya to continue to fast and pray for another three days on the mountain so all the chains of wickedness around her life would be broken. Adannaya responded with a big AMEN! and followed through with all his instructions.

Indeed, God answered Adannaya's prayers and blessed her with a beautiful baby girl. Adannaya named her daughter Esther, following the biblical Esther. This was all Adannaya desired; she was happy, as was Chima. However, Adannaya's joy was short-lived as the domestic abuse she experienced in the marriage intensified. There were days when Adannaya was too scared to return home from work, and she would drive to her cousin Ejike's house in Lekki since it was nearer to her home than her Obioma's house in Surulere. Adannaya started to wonder about her future with Chima and how they would raise a child in that toxic environment.

One day, her brothers visited Adannaya in her home, but Chima was not there as he had perfected the act of being conveniently absent when his in-laws visited.

Akachi and Obioma knew that the terrible and unsafe situation in their sister's matrimonial home had not changed for the better. With Esther in the home, the siblings were more worried for the safety of mother and child because Chima could harm both because of his erratic behaviour. However, they knew Adannaya was not ready to end her marriage, but the brothers had come up with another plan that might be the solution if they could convince their sister to do it. Akachi felt responsible for his sister's predicament because of the role he played in persuading her to marry Chima.

After about twenty minutes of a serious discussion about the need for Adannaya to leave the marriage without success, Akachi stood up to go to the toilet. That was when he noticed a crack on the wall in a corner of the living room. It was quite a bad crack, but you had to be near the wall to notice it. Akachi remembered it wasn't there the last time he visited his sister's home. He immediately became alarmed.

"What is this crack on your wall? What happened here?" Akachi pointed to the spot.

"Oh, that. Chima threw a bottle at me, and I was able to duck to avoid it, and it hit the wall," said Adannaya dismissively, as though it wasn't a big deal.

Obioma and Akachi looked at each other in astonishment. "He threw a bottle at you?" they said at the same time. Akachi shelved going to the toilet.

"Yes, but he has thrown worse things at me. Like soup and even a lamp," Adannaya shrugged.

"Can you hear yourself? You are beginning to normalise his behaviour. You just shrugged it off like it wasn't a big deal," said Akachi sadly.

"No, I am not normalising it," argued Adannaya.

Obioma shook his head in disbelief. "Sis, you just did because it doesn't shock you anymore. You are not the same Adannaya I know. This is not you. The old Adannaya would have left this house long ago.

"But I leave all the time when it becomes too much. Don't I come to your house? Sometimes, I go to Ejike's house nearby," Adannaya asked Obioma.

"That is not what we are talking about because you have been going and coming back. We want you to leave permanently and relocate to the USA," said Akachi, finally revealing their plan to her.

That took Adannaya by surprise. "Relocate to the USA?" She asked.

Obioma jumped in quickly. "Sis, you have to do it for yourself and Esther before this man harms both of you, and you know he is capable of doing it."

"I don't know if…"

"Yes, you know he is capable of it. There are many women who have lost their lives in similar situations. We are not talking about a divorce, so don't worry about that for now. All we want is for you to move abroad so you can both be safe," explained Akachi.

"Okay, I see what you mean." Adannaya liked the idea of relocating abroad if it meant not divorcing her husband. She was not ready to end her marriage yet.

"So, will you do it?" Asked Obioma, feeling some relief already.

"Yes, but not to America. I have been there so many times, and I do not want to live there. I would rather relocate to the UK. I prefer London because I have attended a few training courses there, and I know my way around the underground and bus system in London," Adannaya said, smiling. For the first time since the problems in her marriage began, she could finally see a way out, the light at the end of the tunnel.

"That is okay, so pack your baggage. Let's go to Obioma's house and brainstorm how we can make it happen. There is much to plan."

"Okay, I am coming. Hold Esther for me," said Adannaya as she handed her daughter to Obioma and ran to her room to start packing.

Adannaya was thankful for her brothers' concern for her safety. What would she have done if she did not have them looking out for her.

On their way to Obioma's house, they stopped at their cousin Ejike's house to inform him of the solution they came up with.

Ejike was relieved to hear about the relocation plan because Adannaya had hidden away in his house on a few occasions to get away from her husband.

Ejike knew just how to help Adannaya. He told Adannaya's brothers about a friend of his who had just relocated to Scotland using the Highly Skilled Migrant Programme (HSMP). Adannaya and her brothers agreed it was a brilliant idea and a Godsent opportunity. Ejike introduced his friend to Adannaya, and he guided her on how to make the application.

Adannaya easily qualified for the HSMP migrant visa because of her top job, income, and educational qualifications. She included her husband and daughter in the application for the HSMP visa, which was granted to them. Adannaya knew that the Nigerian patriarchal structure emboldened some men to do whatever they wanted. Adannaya believed that Chima's abusive behaviour would be curtailed if they lived in the UK because the laws and regulations protect women and punish anyone who broke those laws. She was convinced that the fear of the consequences would set her husband straight.

Chima turned down the offer to relocate to the UK. Adannaya appealed to Chima's uncle to intervene and convince Chima to relocate with her. Not even this well-respected uncle Greg could persuade Chima to change his mind. Adannaya was not surprised that her husband refused to relocate with her and his daughter. Chima did not want to be subject to anyone.

Having previously lived in the western world, he was worried that relocating to the UK could lead to a divorce, and he would lose his transformed lifestyle, home, and business. Therefore, he refused to sign the papers for Adannaya to obtain travel documents for Esther in the hope that Adannaya would abandon her relocation plans.

Adannaya ignored her husband and continued with her plans. She struggled with having to leave Esther behind as she was only a year and three months old. Eventually, Adannaya had to leave for the UK. She handed Esther over to her younger sister, Nwanneka, to care for her in the interim and finalized her plans to leave Nigeria.

Adannaya had no choice but to abandon all she had worked so hard to accomplish and travelled without her beloved daughter, whom she prayed for and endured years of abuse from her husband to have. It was an incredibly painful experience for her.

Tears ran down Adannaya's cheeks as she sat on the plane en route to London. She did not recognise herself anymore. How did she become a woman who begged her abusive husband to move abroad with her? To do what? To continue the abuse? After all she had been through? Was that love? Or was she losing her mind? Maybe it was her Christian faith that taught her that God hates divorce and that she must not divorce her husband no matter what. Or was it her Igbo culture that was also against a woman divorcing her husband?

Adannaya realised she had been feeling trapped for a long time in the five years of her marriage. She was extremely unhappy but was unable to get out of the situation. Fleeing repeatedly to the USA, Obioma's house and Ejike's house provided temporary respite, but she always returned.

This time, it was permanent. She had escaped for good. Her only pain was not having her daughter with her, but the knowledge that she was in the loving care of her sister, Nwanneka, was satisfactory. Adannaya had to heal and gather the strength she knew would be required to fight for her daughter. For now, she could finally exhale. She was FREE.

PART TWO

Life In the UK

CHAPTER 6

Escape to the UK

Adannaya took the six-hour flight from Lagos to London. She reminisced about her past and current situation and wondered what the future held for her regarding her marriage and daughter, Esther, back in Nigeria. If only she wasn't embarking on this journey alone. For the umpteenth time, Adannaya wished Esther was with her, held lovingly in her arms. She sighed and crossed her arms to give herself the semblance of a comforting hug.

Adannaya reluctantly allowed her mind to drift to less painful thoughts. She remembered her former colleague and friend, Abigail, who had relocated to the United Kingdom under the HSMP visa scheme a year ago. Abigail used to work at GTTNet but now lived in London. Adannaya was glad she had Abigail, who was in the same migrant program as herself and could give her the information she needed to find her feet in the city and country.

Remembering that she was still in contact with Abigail made the relocation less daunting for Adannaya because she had only been in the UK for short periods on holidays. She had no idea about the requirements for finding a job, renting a place, or opening a local bank account.

On arrival at Heathrow Airport London, Adannaya took the underground train known as the Piccadilly Line to Uncle Tom's house in North London. The house was in Bounds Green, a short distance from the tube station. Perfect for commuting.

When Adannaya arrived at Uncle Tom's house, her relatives were surprised to see her looking very dishevelled and worn out. She did not look like her usual glamorous and happy self. They were concerned and asked her if everything was alright with her. Adannaya explained that she has been unwell but had also been granted HSMP to live and work in the UK.

The next day, Adannaya called her friend, Abigail, and discussed accommodation and job search. Abigail invited Adannaya and proposed that she share her two-bedroom flat in North London. Adannaya was happy to hear that because that was one challenge she could tick off her list, as staying with her relatives was always meant to be a temporary arrangement.

Abigail informed Adannaya that she needed three things to be eligible for employment in the UK. First was the National Insurance number, popularly known as an NI. The second requirement was a permanent address and a local bank account. The third one was the easiest for Adannaya because she already had an international bank account with a high street bank, which she opened in Nigeria courtesy of her well-paid job then. She has a reasonable amount of money in the account. She believed that would simplify the bank account opening process for her.

When Adannaya asked Uncle Tom how to apply for a national insurance number, he was surprised because it was such a difficult item for immigrants to obtain. He did not believe Adannaya would qualify for one despite her explanation that she had a valid work permit visa (HSMP), which afforded her the right to work in the UK.

Uncle Tom could not direct her to apply for the NI. Therefore, Adannaya went back to Abigail again, who explained the application process to her. Adannaya applied for the National insurance number and received it within a week.

When Adannaya showed Uncle Tom her NI card, he almost fell off the sofa in surprise.

"Wow! This is a miracle," he shouted. "Do you know how many years it takes immigrants to get an NI number? Do you know what they have to do to obtain one? They have to pass through difficult hurdles. Unbelievable!"

Adannaya couldn't help laughing at Uncle Tom's reaction and the many questions he was asking her. Clearly, he had experienced some difficulty settling in the UK, but she did not ask him about that. He continued probing further about her relocation plans and processes.

"How did you do it? You this girl, everything you touch turns to gold. How did you do it? Tell me so I can I tell others."

Adannaya could not understand why it was such a big deal, so she shrugged her shoulders as she explained it to him.

"I applied for the HSMP - Highly Skilled Migrant Programme visa while I was still in Nigeria, and I got it before I came here." That elicited an even bigger reaction from him.

"You mean you applied for the right to work in the UK from Nigeria? Wow! I thought you came here with your visitor's visa as usual."

"Yes, I still have my 5-year visitor's visa, but this is a work permit visa. So, I have both visas now."

"How did you apply for it? Which agency did it for you, and how much did you pay for it?" He asked in fascination.

Adannaya explained how Ejike introduced her to his friend who migrated to Scotland under the HSMP visa scheme and how that person taught her how to apply for the visa.

"I did not go through an agent. I applied for it myself, and it cost only the official application fee."

Uncle Tom was now standing because he heard something he never knew was possible, and he was too excited to remain seated.

"Eziokwu? Just like that?"

"Yes, just like that, and I got the visa within 3 months."

Uncle Tom thought it was the most valuable piece of information he had received since he arrived in the UK, and he called his wife to hear what Adannaya was saying. They were both intrigued by the revelation.

Adannaya realised that many immigrants from Nigeria go through excruciating difficulties settling in the UK because of the visa scheme they applied for. Her conversation with Uncle Tom revealed the lack of information on the available visa schemes for work permits and residency. She was glad that she was able to share this information about the HSMP with her relatives because she knew they would spread the news far and wide to the benefit of many Nigerians.

As days passed, Adannaya needed to get some money to cover her living expenses. Adannaya was not bothered about it because she had a tidy sum of money in her international bank account with one of the UK high street banks. She had a fixed deposit investment with the bank that was maturing soon.

Adannaya went to the bank with the intention of withdrawing some money from her account. To her disbelief, they did not recognise her, and it was because of how different she looked. The bank officials did not believe that the dishevelled and miserable-looking woman standing before them was the same Adannaya Ugwumba, their ever-glamorous customer and account owner. Not even the fact that she was holding the same Nigerian international passport with which she opened the bank account and the latest bank statement sent to her was sufficient proof that she was the legitimate account holder. Adannaya argued this point until she was blue in the face, but they did not believe her.

Adannaya did not know what to do but knew who to go to for advice on a problem like this. It had to be

Abigail. As a fellow HSMP migrant, she would know the best course of action.

Adannaya was not disappointed. Abigail knew exactly what to do. She advised Adannaya to call the bank and threaten them that if they did not grant her access to her account and release her money, then they would be responsible for anything that happened to her in the UK because she had no other means of survival. Adannaya was hesitant. How could she say such a thing to the bank, she wondered. However, Abigail was able to convince her that it was the only way to get the bank's attention.

Adannaya gave in and did as she was told, and that changed everything. It was like magic because the bank officers did not sound like the same rude and unhelpful people. They asked Adannaya to come to the bank the next day so the matter could be resolved.

Adannaya was at the bank very early the next day. They gave her immediate cash as her fixed deposit had matured. Then, they opened a local bank account for her and transferred all her money into it.

When Adannaya informed Uncle Tom and his wife about the bank account, they were amazed once again at how quickly and easily Adannaya was able to achieve that. Now that she had access to her money, she was ready to move out. Adannaya spent about three weeks with her relatives before she moved out, but she kept in touch with them and visited them when she could.

Adannaya moved in with Abigail, and they became flatmates in the two-bedroom flat in Northwest London.

Adannaya had been eager to start job hunting, and now that she had the three things she needed to find work in the UK (the national insurance number, a local bank account, and a permanent address), she did exactly that.

Adannaya believed she would find a job quickly, considering she was a high-flying top executive in the telecommunications sector. Based on that, Adannaya prepared her CV to highlight her exceptional performance, skills, qualifications, and experience. She applied to telecommunications companies in the UK and hoped to get a similar role in one of those companies. To her surprise and disappointment, she wasn't shortlisted for any interviews, and when she enquired, she was told she was overqualified for the roles she applied for. She applied through all the online recruitment agencies she could find, but her applications were rejected for all the roles.

Abigail, who had been in the UK for a year, was still struggling to secure a decent permanent job, so she was unable to provide the right guidance. Abigail only had temporary jobs with agencies but no permanent jobs.

While Adannaya was dealing with this unemployment challenge, she continued providing for Esther by sending money to Nwanneka for Esther's upkeep. Adannaya sent money regularly and bought excellent quality clothes from some of the best clothing retailers for her daughter. Esther had a nanny and was already attending nursery school, which meant additional expenses for Adannaya as Chima did not provide any financial support. He was now focused on providing for his teenage mistress and their child. Adannaya also spent a lot of money on phone calls to Nigeria because of the expensive calling cards, as this was what was available then.

Adannaya was lucky to befriend some fellow Nigerian immigrants in her neighbourhood at Colindale, where she lived, and they introduced her to the sale of Avon products. Adannaya could not be idle while looking for a job, so she was thankful for the opportunity to become an Avon products agent. She did the business with total commitment. Adannaya ordered massive quantities of Avon products and sold them in London and also in Nigeria.

The Nigeria side of the Avon sales was handled by Adannaya's sister, Nwanneka. Adannaya sent suitcase loads of Avon products to Nwanneka to sell and invest the proceeds in Esther's care and educational expenses.

After a couple of months of unsuccessful job searches, Adannaya began to apply for more junior roles but with the same high-achieving CV and qualifications. It made no difference, and she hit a brick wall once again. She was told several times that she was overqualified for such positions. On one occasion, she secured a telephone interview with one of the UK's big telecom companies but was rejected because, according to them, she had a strong African accent, which was not acceptable.

Soon, Adannaya realized that she was applying for jobs in the UK using the Nigerian job-seeking strategies. No one told her she had to use a different strategy and approach to her job search.

Fortunately for Adannaya, she reconnected with the UK branch of her Nigerian church, and they welcomed her and gave her the much-needed support and guidance with her job search in the UK. These were the UNTOLD RULES and strategies that most immigrants never learnt until after months of struggling and inability to find work in the UK. Adannaya was no different and only found out about these strategies after three months. She wrote them in her journal,

- *Remove degree qualifications and managerial experience of senior roles when applying for ju-*

nior roles because it is apparent that you are overqualified for such roles. Very few employers will hire a graduate or master's degree holder for the role of a Sales Assistant or Customer Service Representative. With such qualifications, the employer knows the candidates are unlikely to remain in that job for long and would resign as soon as something better comes along.

- *UK work experience is required. The sooner one can gain UK experience that can provide an employment reference, the better. Even if it means taking on voluntary work, it is worth it to gain that experience.*
- *Stick to the job description for application and at interviews, and do not mention the amazing things you did in other jobs that may be irrelevant to the job being interviewed for. In addition, the CV must be tailored to fit the role.*
- *Avoid the mistake made by many newly arrived immigrants of focusing on the managerial jobs they had done in their career history rather than trying to convince the interview panel that they were a good fit for the role they applied for.*
- *The application method for jobs in the public sector was different from those in the private sector. Sending a CV to the recruiter or employ-*

er is usually acceptable for private-sector jobs. Applying for public sector jobs requires completing many forms. Without the submission of this form, the applicant will not be shortlisted for an interview.

These very valuable nuggets of advice were the game changer for Adannaya. If only someone had told her about them months ago. She immediately amended her CV and removed the degrees and postgraduate qualifications from it, as well as her work experience in senior roles. She kept her junior roles as an advertising executive and customer service representative.

Adannaya prioritised securing a part-time volunteer job to gain work experience in the UK. Her first job in Lagos at the Crime Detective magazine became her competitive advantage, and she was able to get a volunteer job as a sub-editor for the magazine.

The magazine was linked with a much-loved and charismatic former Labours prime minister and promoted the amazing charity work that he was doing. Adannaya found the job extremely exciting because she met the former prime minister and many of the famous top Labours Party leaders. As a volunteer, the only payment Adannaya received was travel and lunch allowance. She enjoyed the job, and it piqued Adannaya's interest in politics and the Labours Party.

Adannaya continued to sell her Avon products while doing her volunteer work. She also continued searching for a paid job. Adannaya shared the job search strategy with Abigail, and she was able to secure a customer service job at Middlesex Council. After three months at the job, Abigail found out about a part-time job opportunity in her department and quickly introduced Adannaya to the recruitment agency that got her own job.

Adannaya was well prepared this time because she knew the DOs and DONTs of seeking employment in the UK. She got the job, and it was Adannaya's first paid job in the UK. It was a part-time job of three days a week (twenty-two hours), and Adannaya spent the other two days of the week doing volunteer work for the magazine.

One day, Adannaya's pastor's wife in the London church asked Adannaya if she would like to do a night job for two nights a week. The role was a support worker at a residential home for adults with learning disability. Her pastor's wife was the deputy manager of the home, which made it easy to know when there was an opening.

Adannaya gladly accepted it because it was another paid job.

With both paid jobs, Adannaya could earn enough wages equivalent to a full-time salary. Adannaya was finally able to stop both her volunteer work and her sales of Avon products.

It took about nine months for Adannaya to finally settle down in the UK with paid jobs. She had spent months volunteering and selling Avon products, but she got there in the end. Now that Adannaya was earning enough money to prove she could provide for her daughter, Esther, in the UK, she could kick-start bringing her daughter to the UK as soon as possible.

CHAPTER

7

Fighting For Esther

Adannaya was constantly preoccupied with thoughts of how to bring her daughter, Esther, to the UK. It was all she could think about or talk about. Luckily for her, she received good advice on how to prepare for Esther's visa application from the people that fate brought her way. One person Adannaya met at training was a fellow Nigerian who listened to her story and saw how pained she was about being away from her only child. He advised her not to be hasty about making the visa application because it might be rejected. After all, she had not had a permanent job for at least six months. That was one of the requirements to prove she could provide for her daughter. He also advised her to keep all the receipts of clothes she bought for Esther and the fund's transfer acknowledgement of the money she sent for Esther's care and education in Nigeria. Adannaya went a step further and kept all the email correspondence she sent to her sister, Nwanneka, who was looking after Esther in Nigeria.

In addition, Adannaya applied to the Surestart Children Centre (the early education government centre) to secure nursery admission for Esther pending her move to the UK.

Adannaya successfully secured admission for Esther and decided it was the right time to submit another application for Esther to be issued a visa to join her in London. It would be her second visa application. The first time Adannaya applied for her daughter's visa was before she left Nigeria, and her application was rejected because Chima did not consent to Adannaya's relocation with Esther to the UK.

The initial HSMP application approval was for Adannaya to relocate to the UK with her husband and child. Therefore, they failed to understand why Adannaya requested to leave the country with her daughter without her husband's consent.

Adannaya made a second application; this time, she provided relevant documents to evidence of how she had provided for Esther and planned to care for her in the UK. Nwanneka helped to submit the visa application to the British High Commission in Lagos on behalf of Adannaya. Once again, the application was rejected. Adannaya decided to file an appeal against the decision, and a friend advised her to file the appeal in the UK because it would improve her chances of success.

She supported her application with a thick folder full of documentary evidence. She made duplicate copies of every document she submitted with the intention of taking them to court with her.

Adannaya turned up in court without a lawyer because she wanted to represent herself. It was her case and her life. She believed no lawyer could plead her case better and with the required passion it deserved than herself. She came prepared with all her documentary evidence and all the love she had for her daughter in her heart. She was simply a mum fighting for her child. Adannaya prayed fervently that the judge would feel for her and rule the case in her favour.

The documents she submitted also included evidence of everything that went on in her marriage: the physical violence and abuse, her husband impregnating a teenage domestic staff, etc. Additionally, there was evidence of how she was supporting her daughter financially in Nigeria and plans for her when she arrived in the UK. Adannaya was confident that the documents she had would help her case.

The court clerk called the case, and Adannaya sat down on the opposite side of the Home Office legal team. They were all facing the female judge and waited for the hearing to begin.

The Judge addressed Adannaya.

"Where is your lawyer?" Asked the judge.

"I am representing myself, My Lord."

The Judge nodded and invited the home office lawyers to present the case to the court, and they did.

"What do you have to say, Mrs Mbadiwe?" The judge probed.

Adannaya replied, "My Lord, may I approach you? I want to unzip my trousers a little bit to show you something.

The judge was surprised to hear that.

"What is it?"

"I want to show you my tummy so you can see the marks and scars of different operations I had undergone in the process of seeking to have a child."

"There is no need for that, I believe you."

"Thank you, my Lord. I have heard what the Home Office lawyer said, and the only thing I will say is this - if you reject this appeal, my Lord, you are saying that I should return to Nigeria because I cannot live here without my daughter. My body and my soul cannot accept it. And if I must go back to Nigeria, I will fight with my last breath and will continue to appeal until I have exhausted all the options that are available to me before I go back to Nigeria."

The judge asked the home office lawyer if they had anything else to say, and they responded by quoting all the sections of the law to support their decision to reject Adannaya's application, and it was simply because her husband, Chima, did not give his consent for their daughter to be taken out of the country by her mother. Since both parents have parental responsibility over the child, his consent was required.

The judge opened Adannaya's big folder, which accompanied her application, and started perusing it.

"I have been on this job for twenty years, and I cannot understand why so many African women try to protect a marriage that does not exist. Mrs Mbadiwe, as educated and as exposed as you are, why are you trying to protect a marriage that no longer exists?"

"My lord, Where I come from, a marriage is not only about the couple. A marriage unites two families, two villages, two towns, two churches or two mosques, etc..."

"Yes, I have heard that, and I understand..." The judge interjected.

"Yes, my Lord, these structures support the marriage and work hard to protect it from collapsing. In many cases, it works for good, but sometimes, some people find themselves in dead marriages despite their educational level or exposure."

"Mrs Mbadiwe, you are very insightful."

"Thank you, my Lord," she responded.

"Now, let's look at the fact of the matter. Did you calculate that your husband must have been messing with that teenage domestic staff long before she became pregnant?"

"Yes, I now realise that, my Lord."

The Judge and Adannaya sounded like two colleagues at work having a private conversation instead of people at a court hearing.

"I have come to a conclusion," the judge finally said.

She turned to the home office lawyers.

"Let me share my story," she began. I recently had twins. One day, I asked my husband to look after one of our twins while I cared for the other. Could you guess how long my husband could take care of our child for?"

No one dared to answer the judge, so she continued.

"He could only manage for ten minutes before he started pleading with me to come and take the baby, and he asked me to forgive him now and for any future offences."

The women in the courtroom smiled, and the men looked down to hide their expressions.

"The reason I am saying this is because I do not understand how the Home Office can look at a woman like you and say you can't look after her 2-year-old baby."

The judge looked through Adannaya's file once again. She stated all the wonderful things Adannaya had done for her daughter: the expenses, receipts for clothes she bought, payment for the nursery, hospital bills paid, fund transfer confirmation, etc. When the judge came to the Unit Trust investments, she was left in awe of Adannaya.

"This woman has been making fifty pounds worth of Unit Trust investments every month for her daughter, who is in Nigeria. I am a mother in the UK with my kids here, and I have not yet bought unit trust investments for any of them. So, what other proof of commitment do you need from this woman?"

Adannaya smiled for the first time and started to feel hopeful that she could win the appeal. The judge continued to address the home office lawyers.

"But you Home Office are happy to leave the child with an abuser of a teenage domestic staff instead of an incredibly loving mother?"

The judge mentioned the email Adannaya sent to her sister, asking her to convince Chima to come for Esther's birthday so that their daughter would not feel isolated from both her parents. The home office lawyers looked uncomfortable because they could see that their case was falling apart.

"This is my judgement," the judge pronounced. "I am going to do something I have never done before. We are in May. If the child is not in the UK with her mother by September, then I am not a judge. Court dismissed!"

As the judge walked past Adannaya, she said, "You will get my judgment."

Adannaya was in shock and confused. "Has she agreed? Is everything okay now?"

Since Adannaya did not know much about a UK court's modus operandi, comprehending what had just happened took her a while. There were lots of hugs and congratulations from the home office lawyers and other people in the court. It finally dawned on Adannaya that she had won her appeal against the home office decision.

Tears of joy and relief rolled down Adannaya's cheeks. She could not believe the good news. She was shaking and sweating at the same time. That day was one of the happiest days of her life.

When Adannaya received the judgment from the judge a few weeks later, it was eighteen pages long. Indeed, the judge's ruling was extraordinary. Adannaya whooped with joy and danced around her room again, singing her usual favourite gospel song:

'What The LORD has done for me. I cannot tell it all.'

The judgement stated that Adannaya must go to Nigeria and bring Esther to the UK herself and that no one else was allowed to bring Esther over. Adannaya loved that and was soon on a flight to Nigeria.

At the British High Commission in Lagos, Adannaya was pleasantly surprised to discover that they were already expecting her because the judge had written to them about Adannaya's case. They issued Esther's visa speedily, and Adannaya collected it. Adannaya did not share the good news with many people, and it was important that she kept it confidential until she was safely out of the country with her daughter.

Now that Adannaya had Esther's UK visa sorted, she travelled to NdiOrlu to spend a few days with her mother, whom she had not seen for a while since Adannaya moved in the UK. Mrs Ugwumba woke Adannaya up at night to discuss the Esther situation.

"Nne, what are you going to do about your daughter?" Mrs Ugwumba cried, and she continued. "What are you going to do o! Eh, nne! Ewo!"

Mrs Ugwumba paused to wipe her tears and resumed weeping and lamenting.

"That man said you will never take that child. He said he would never sign! What are you going to do o?"

"Mama, it is okay," Adannaya tried to calm her mother down.

"How can you lose everything, eh? You lost all your properties and are now about to lose your only child. What kind of bad luck is this one nau! You that all of us used to see as light o! What kind of darkness is revolving around you like this, eh!" Mrs Ugwumba wept uncontrollably.

Adannaya wished she could tell her mother the truth to put her out of her misery, but she could not tell her the good news yet. Nonetheless, she knew what to say to reassure her mother.

"Mama?"

"Yes?"

"If I do not take her to London, then you will know that the God we serve is no longer Omnipotent," said Adannaya emphatically.

Her mother was relieved. She stopped crying. "Ehe! Is that so?"

"Yes! God will do it. Don't cry. God will resolve this matter. God is still in heaven. Don't worry."

"Okay, I trust you, my daughter."

After that, they both went back to bed.

Adannaya also paid a visit to her uncle, who echoed the concerns previously raised by her mother. This was expected, as she was aware that her entire family had been concerned about her since her marital issues began. Adannaya assured him, as she did for her mum, that God would resolve the matter. He agreed and encouraged her to pray more.

A week later, Adannaya boarded the flight to London with Esther. She hugged her precious daughter close. She had dreamt of this moment many times, prayed about it, fantasised about it, and now that it had finally happened, the reality was even better than the dream. She was ecstatic with joy. It was everything she wanted, and now Esther was coming home with her.

Adannaya was beside herself with joy, and Esther could feel it, too. She hugged her mum tightly and held onto her. Adannaya decided it was a suitable time to finally share the good news with her mum.

At her home in London, Adannaya called her mother and passed the phone to Esther. Mrs Ugwumba was surprised to hear Esther's voice on the international call because she did not know Adannaya left with Esther. Adannaya told her mum everything, and Mrs Ugwumba screamed with excitement. Adannaya could hear her mother singing and dancing with joy. The relief in her mother's voice was palpable, and Adannaya asked her to inform her uncle and the rest of the family that they had nothing to worry about anymore because she was safely back in London with her daughter.

A few days later, Adannaya received a phone call from the British High Commission in Nigeria. It was a male voice.

"Hello, is that Mrs Mbadiwe?"

"Hello, yes, please."

"I am calling from the British High Commission in Nigeria."

Adannaya wasn't expecting a call from them and wondered why they had called her.

"Okay? How can I help you, please?"

“Don’t be alarmed. We are only calling to confirm that Esther has arrived safely in London with you?”

“Oh, okay!” Adannaya grinned. “Yes, Esther is here with me. We arrived earlier this earlier week.”

“Wow, that is great.”

“May I ask why you called to confirm?”

“We are simply following the instructions of the judge. She requested that we call to confirm Esther’s arrival.”

“Wow! I understand. Thank you. Everything is fine now. My daughter is finally here with me.”

“Can we speak to Esther?”

“Of course. Esther, come and say hello,” Adannaya gave her daughter the phone.

Three-year-old Esther took the phone from her mum.

“H-e-w-o! H-e-w-o!” She said excitedly, like any toddler given a phone to use.

“Hello Esther, how are you?”

“F-i-n-e.”

Adannaya took the phone back from her daughter. “Was that sufficient proof?”

“Yes, it is. Sorry, we had to be sure.”

“No need to apologise. I am glad you called to confirm, and I can see how thorough you are.”

"Now, we can report to the judge that this matter can be closed."

Adannaya agreed with him. "Of course. Let's close it. It is done now. Thank you very much."

"You are welcome, Mrs Mbadiwe"

"My regards to the judge, please."

"Okay. Goodbye"

"Bye!"

With Esther now in the UK with her, Adannaya was able to focus all her attention on building a great life for both of them. First, she took Esther to the Sure start centre to continue her nursery education. Next, she took the UK driving test to qualify for a driver's license. Adannaya soon secured a mortgage, and they moved to their first home in Becking.

The natural next step for Adannaya was to get herself out of the non-existent marriage, as the judge said. She kept replaying her conversation with the Judge in her head and knew her divorce was going to be an uphill task because all the systems would try to prevent it, but in her characteristic doggedness, Adannaya was determined to give it a go.

She filed for divorce through a law firm in Nigeria, and the battle began. As soon as the divorce papers were filed, she was inundated with phone calls from Chima's family pleading with her to withdraw the application for divorce. Chima's uncle, the traditional ruler, said, "Whatever it will take, we will resolve it. How can you think about divorce?"

Adannaya's extended family also got involved and asked her to withdraw the case. Some pleaded, and others admonished Adannaya. The pressure was unbelievable! All the uncles and relatives from both sides of the family got involved. There were many family meetings and village meetings to discuss how to stop the divorce. Obioma and Nwanneka were among the few who stood by her. Even though her extended family members knew how terrible her marriage to Chima was and the horrific things he did to her, they asked her not to divorce him. Many blamed it on her relocation to the UK, which they believed had filled her head with bad ideas, such as divorcing her husband.

Adannaya's uncle said, "What did I hear? That you filed for divorce? This white man's mentality has entered your brain, eh! This Obodoyibo! Obodoyibo!"

Adannaya could see that her community accepted her separation from Chima, and they were happy for her to remain in that situation as long as she never formally divorced her husband. Adannaya wondered what type of life that was for any woman. How can a woman be married but single?

Meanwhile, Chima was playing "happy family" with another traditionally married woman who was now the mother of his children and his teenage mistress who had a daughter for him. Chima fought harder than anyone else to prevent the divorce. He was very manipulative and visited members of both families and even Adannaya's pastor in Nigeria. He wept and begged them to intervene and save his marriage with Adannaya. He claimed his actions were the works of the devil. Adannaya found it hilarious, but it was no surprise to her.

Anyone familiar with their marriage could see that Chima was fighting not just for Adannaya but also to keep the properties, businesses, and lifestyle he gained from their union. He knew he could lose all of it if the marriage ended.

Adannaya's Pastor summoned her for an urgent meeting and said, "What God has joined together, no man should put asunder. A born-again Christian like you should know that."

When she persisted, many of her fellow church members despised her. Some concluded that she had lost her faith due to living in a very liberal and permissive society like the UK.

The divorce courts in Nigeria were another obstacle. They kept adjourning the case, which dragged on for three years, costing Adannaya a lot of money.

Unsurprisingly, this was very frustrating, expensive, and stressful for Adannaya as she had to deal with this for over three years from the UK. One day, she mentioned her divorce woes to a work colleague, and luckily, her colleague was well-informed and had some valuable information to share with Adannaya.

She told Adannaya that if a married couple is separated for five years, the divorce would almost be automatic if they filed in the UK. Adannaya sighed with relief because her separation from Chima would be five years long in just a few months.

When that time came, Adannaya engaged a London law firm to handle the divorce. Within months, Adannaya received the Decree Nisi and later the Decree Absolute, and that finalised the divorce. It was a sad end to a holiday romance. Nonetheless, she felt liberated to face her future.

Though Adannaya's court marriage had been dissolved, she was still married traditionally to Chima. In her culture, until her bride's price was returned by her family to Chima's, and they accepted it, she remained his wife. Chima knew that though he was now married to another woman traditionally and had a mistress, it was very acceptable that he could be a polygamist. It was no surprise to see Chima attending family events in the Ugwumba family and still behaving like a son-in-law despite not being invited.

Adannaya was uncomfortable with the situation and persuaded her family to return the dowry. They were reluctant to do so, especially Akachi. Adannaya tried all she could, and eventually, her uncle accepted her decision and agreed to help. They contacted the official witness at the traditional marriage, who was the person mandated by tradition to return the dowry. When he took the dowry back, the Mbadiwe family refused to accept it because Chima had warned them never to accept the money. Adannaya's family offered to pay four times the original bride price to facilitate the process in case of any additional expense. That did not work either because Chima and his family rejected the dowry once again.

Adannaya was at a loss and unsure of what to do next. She prayed to God for a solution because she knew divine intervention was what she needed at that point. Her prayers were answered because Adannaya and her family learned that the state government had passed a new law that allowed a woman and her family to register the rejected dowry at the Local Government Office, and they would be issued a receipt as an acknowledgment that the bride price had been returned. A copy of the receipt would then be sent to the husband's family.

Adannaya's family did just that, and it marked the end of the marriage between Adannaya Ugwumba and Chima Mbadiwe.

Adannaya was baffled by what she had to go through to get a divorce. She wondered if she would have gone through this ordeal if she was a man. She questioned whether the traditional Igbo culture, where a woman is typically under the authority of either her father or husband, contributes to the marginalization of women. Alternatively, she considered whether the interaction between religion and culture tends to treat women as second-class citizens. She wondered what would have been her fate if this new law had not been implemented to help women like her get through the different layers of tortures divorce proceedings in one marriage.

CHAPTER 8

Gateway Into the World of Politics

After her divorce, Adannaya reflected on her life's journey and began to contemplate her future and career.

She observed the social workers who came regularly to review the care of the service users she supported when she did night shifts at the learning disability home where she worked. She picked interest in their role, particularly how they advocated for their service users and ensured their rights were respected. They made a great impression on Adannaya.

Adannaya was intrigued by the structure of the UK government for supporting the vulnerable in society. Where she came from, the family and community shoulder this responsibility. She decided to make inquiries about the profession of social work and eligibility criteria. Adannaya did a skills audit with a career adviser, and the result confirmed that her skills and attributes were better aligned with advocating for people, ensuring that people's rights are protected, and helping people make the most out of their lives.

In her characteristic determination, Adannaya did her research and began the process of gaining admission into one of the UK universities to do a master's degree in social work. She applied for her transcript from Nigeria, and it arrived in good time.

The admission process was rigorous as she had to undergo a 3-stage interview process, which included assessments, a group interview, and a one-on-one interview. Adannaya applied to Brunei University, London, and the University of Buckinghamshire. She gained admission to both universities and chose Brunei University because it had a good reputation for social work and was nearer home. Brunei gave Adannaya an International Student admission as her immigration status was still a work permit under HMSP. Adannaya was worried about losing this admission as she could not afford the expensive international school fees. She prayed fervently to God for intervention and contacted the university admissions team, explaining her circumstances. The university confirmed to her that if she were a home student, she would qualify for a scholarship due to her excellent performance in the assessment.

The funding was only available to home students, and since Adannaya was an international student, the university could not award her the scholarship. Adannaya was determined to find a solution and prayed to God to help her find a way. However, her HSMP visa had some months left before she could qualify for permanent residency or INDEFINITE LEAVE TO REMAIN (ILR), as it is popularly known. Adannaya trusted God to intervene in her situation.

The rules regarding the application for ILR stipulated that Adannaya could apply within three months of the visa expiration, and Adannaya decided to take advantage of that to avoid losing the university admission. Time was of the essence. Instead of making the usual postal application, Adannaya was proactive and decided to apply in person to get a quicker response.

On the day, Adannaya took Esther with her, and together, they boarded a train and went straight to the Home Office in Croydon, London. Adannaya's application was processed there, and she was awarded permanent residency for Esther and herself. Their fingerprints and biometrics were processed, and a letter stating Adannaya's successful ILR application was issued to her.

While Adannaya was waiting for the biometric card to arrive, she sent that ILR visa award letter to the university, and they put Adannaya's name forward for the scholarship. Adannaya was awarded a full scholarship, and she was grateful to the UK because that scholarship paid not only her school fees but also everything she needed for her upkeep, including childcare costs. When she read the scholarship letter and saw the amount of funding in her award, she was very surprised. She considered herself incredibly lucky to be in that fortunate position.

Adannaya was very pleased about this and was relieved that she could focus on her studies without any worries about her finances.

Adannaya became a university student once again; this time, she was a mother with a child in school. As Adannaya went to school, so did Esther. Esther attended the biggest primary school in Becking.

Something happened in the school one day when Esther was about six years old. She had an argument with a classmate. She decided the best thing to do was to get some photos from her mother to show her classmates. When she arrived home, she went straight to it.

"Mummy?"

"Yes, dear"

"Can I have a photo of our house in Nigeria?" Asked Esther.

Adannaya assumed it was for school homework like 'SHOW AND TELL' and that Esther's teacher must have asked them to bring it, so she gave Esther the photos. However, Adannaya's curiosity got the better of her.

"What do you need the photos for?" she asked.

"Oh, I want to show my classmates that we have big, beautiful houses in Nigeria.

"Oh really!"

"Yes mummy," answered Esther, smiling.

That was not the reply her mother expected to hear, but she shrugged and gave Esther the photos. Adannaya forgot all about it.

A few days later, while Adannaya was on placement as part of her social work programme, she received a call from Esther's school. The call was from the deputy head teacher.

"Hello, Esther's mum. I am the school Deputy head teacher, Mrs Abbot," said the woman on the phone.

"Hello, Mrs Abbot. Is Esther okay?" Adannaya was worried.

"Don't worry, your daughter is okay, but there's been a little incident."

Adannaya was worried the more. "A little incident?"

"Yes, there has been a little incident," repeated Mrs Abbot.

"Is my daughter alright?"

"Yeah, yeah!"

Adannaya did not like the reluctant sound in her voice. "What happened?

"Um…um… Esther is upset because another pupil said something that upset her."

"What did the child say?"

"The boy said something about Esther being different."

"What do you mean being different? What does that mean?"

"They were in the playground, and a particular boy refused to play with Esther because she is black."

"Ah! Whaaaat?!" Adannaya exclaimed in surprise. Her supervisor, sitting on the opposite side of the room, heard Adannaya's exclamation, saw the surprised expression on her face, and beckoned her over to know what was happening. Adannaya ended the call with the deputy head teacher and promised to call her back.

Adannaya narrated everything to her supervisor, and she was very understanding and empathetic. Adannaya asked for permission to leave immediately for her daughter's school, and her supervisor agreed that it made perfect sense.

Adannaya drove to the school immediately. At the school reception, Adannaya requested to see the deputy head teacher, Mrs Abbot, and was shown to her office. Mrs Abbot was not expecting Esther's mother, Adannaya, to be at the school but managed to hide her surprise and tried to reassure Adannaya that Esther was okay.

Adannaya needed to see her daughter to ensure she was no longer upset, so she asked for Esther to be brought to her. Esther was happy to see her mother and ran to hug her. Adannaya held her daughter in her arms and asked if she was okay. Esther smiled and told her mother that she was fine. Adannaya asked Esther to return to her classroom.

Adannaya went back to Mrs Abbot to have the necessary conversation.

"Please, can you explain what happened again? It is still a bit confusing to me," asked Adannaya.

Mrs Abbot repeated her narration of the incident.

"So, what happened after that?"

"Esther was upset and reported the boy who said he would not play with her because she is black."

"And how old is this boy?

" Same age as Esther. Five to six years old," answered Mrs Abbot.

"So what did the school do? What is going to happen now?"

"Actually, Esther said that they should call the boy and that she would tell him off.'

Adannaya was not only surprised but also impressed and proud of her daughter. "Really?"

"Yes," answered Mrs Abbot.

"Esther did that?"

"Yes, she did. We summoned the boy, and Esther told him off. To quote Esther, she said, 'why are you saying that? Because in Africa, we have big, beautiful houses."

Adannaya could not help smiling with pride at her daughter's confidence and intelligence. Now she understood why Esther asked for those photos.

As far as Adannaya was concerned, the matter was not yet settled. "I think there is another telling off that needs to happen."

Mrs Abbot became uncomfortable. "What do you mean?"

"A five- or six-year-old boy saying this to his classmate, one wonders where he learned such racism from. Is it from school or at home? He must have learned it from somewhere. That is why there is another telling off that needs to be done," explained Adannaya.

Mrs Abbot was shaken by that. "Oh, please. We have spoken to the boy's parents, and they are really sorry about the incident."

Mrs Abbot was apologetic and pleaded with Adannaya to let it go.

"I will come back tomorrow to make a formal complaint. For now, I want to take my child home because it is coming to the end of school time".

"That's okay, madam," said Mrs Abbot.

At home, Adannaya commended her daughter for being so brave and standing up to a bully. Esther was happy that her mother said she was amazingly brave, and the six-year-old jumped up and down around the room gleefully, which also made her mother happy.

The next day, Adannaya returned to the school to make a proper complaint, just as she had informed Mrs Abbot that she would.

When Adannaya arrived at the school, she asked to see the head teacher this time and had to wait in the reception. As she sat there, she observed the photos on the wall and noted that all the school governors were of Caucasian descent. None of them were black like Adannaya. Wow! None of them looked like me, she thought to herself.

At that moment, the head teacher came out to meet Adannaya, and when she learned why she came to see her, she took Adannaya into her office, offered her a seat, and apologised to Adannaya immediately.

Adannaya was suddenly keen to put the matter behind her and discuss something more significant.

"No, no, let's leave that for a moment. Can I ask you a question?"

"Of course!" Said the head teacher eagerly.

"When are you recruiting for your next batch of school governors?" Adannaya wanted to know.

"Actually, we just finished recruiting our school governors, but if somebody resigns, you know, people normally get tired because it is a voluntary role, and they move on to other things, then we have to get a replacement."

"If one of the school governors resigns, please let me know because I'm interested."

"That would be great. If somebody resigns, we advertise for it immediately. That's how we deal with it."

"Once somebody resigns, or if there's any change and you need to recruit another batch, please let me know," reiterated Adannaya.

"I promise you will be the first to know," assured the head teacher.

As Adannaya got up to leave, the head teacher was surprised that this was all Adannaya wanted to discuss with her.

"Don't you want to talk about why you came here?" The headteacher had to ask.

"No, no, don't worry about it," said Adannaya, and she left.

A few months later, the school advertised for a new parent governor, and Adannaya was notified. Three parents applied for the role, and Adannaya was one of them. Interviews were conducted as part of the selection process, and eventually, Adannaya emerged as the successful candidate. Adannaya became a school governor, and her photo was displayed at the school reception along with the other school governors.

For many months, Adannaya worked hard, embraced her role as a school governor, and served in various capacities. Since she was studying social work, she also took the role of a safeguarding governor.

Adannaya was later appointed as the year six link governor. As part of her remit, she arranged a link governor visit to her year six class. The teacher introduced Adannaya to the class, and she started speaking to the children. They were all sitting in clusters as they often did in primary schools. Adannaya noticed there was only one black boy and a black girl in the classroom.

Adannaya spoke to the children, encouraging them to behave well and explaining all the changes the school was making and how it would benefit them. Adannaya was trying to motivate the pupils. As she was getting to the end of her speech, the year six teacher interjected to say this:

"If anybody has a question for the governor, you can ask now."

Adannaya noticed how quickly the only black girl in the class raised her hand.

The teacher said, "Okay, go on, go on, and ask your question."

The girl smiled and said, "Where are you from?"

Adannaya replied, "Where I'm from?" in surprise.

"Yes," said the black girl.

"I'm from Becking here."

"No, where are you from? Where are you from?" Asked the girl repeatedly.

Adannaya thought she meant where she lived. "I live just across the road from this school, and I can even see the school from my window."

"Auntie, where are you originally from?"

"Okay, is that what you mean? I am originally from Nigeria but live in Becking now".

The moment the black girl heard that Adannaya was originally from Nigeria, she stood up from her seat and began to dance. She whispered to the classmates at her table that Adannaya looked like her mother and spoke like her, too. Her classmates sitting close to her table joined her in the dance. The girl was visibly happy.

Adannaya was quite surprised at the girl's reaction and wondered what must have happened to her to make her react the way she did. Adannaya was humbled and honoured to know that her presence as a school governor could elicit such joy and emotion in a young child from her ethnic group. Adannaya realised just how important her role was to many like that girl.

Adannaya stood there watching the girl in amazement. When she was about to leave, she hugged the girl, wrote her number, and gave it to her.

"What is your name?"

"Shola"

"That is a beautiful name."

"Thank you, Auntie."

"Shola, when you get home today, give this to your mum. Tell her that you saw me and that if you have any problem in this school, she should call my number."

Shola was so happy and thanked Adannaya once again before she departed.

Adannaya had a similar experience once again the following year as a trustee governor of another school, and it was incredibly moving and inspiring for her. The incidents and the school bullying experienced by her daughter, Esther, remained on Adannaya's mind, and she continued to think about them.

In addition, her role as a school governor exposed her to vital information about the schools where she served. For example, Adannaya knew Esther's school had the highest number of children on Pupil premium, which meant that these children were on free school meals due to their parents receiving state support in the form of benefits. Adannaya was also privy to information about the schools' attainment rates, and she could see the disparity between the white and ethnic minority children and looked after children on the league table.

Adannaya could see the level of inequality around her, and that ignited her passion for advocacy. She wondered how she could challenge such inequality. It brought back memories of her all-time career hopes, which was to work with UNICEF. Adannaya thought that this was probably the reason skill audit with the National Career Centre revealed her penchant for advocacy. It was all she wanted to do in life, and that advocacy rose in her again. Adannaya began to think of what she could do to improve the lives of many of these children.

Fortunately, fate had already placed her in a position to prepare her for advocacy. Firstly, she was a school governor with all the experiences and knowledge that came with the position. Secondly, Adannaya was studying social work, which involved a lot of social policy courses that were challenging the status quo on how to improve the society and ensure equality and fairness to empower individuals to exercise their right to self-determination.

All of these made Adannaya more eager to actualise her plans for advocacy, and she started looking for ways to do just that. Unbeknownst to Adannaya, these underlying motivations were the perfect gateway into the world of politics and the opportunity she needed to advance her potential.

CHAPTER 9

Against All Odds

Adannaya continued to think about how she could improve outcomes for children in the local school. At the same time, she was also battling with searching for another school for Esther because she felt that Esther needed to change to a school that was more diverse, and she now came to the conclusion that a faith school would be a good option to help in her quest to give her daughter a solid Christian foundation.

Adannaya applied for an in-year transfer to one of the faith schools through the county council for Esther, but it was rejected because the school was an outstanding school and massively oversubscribed. They did put Esther on a waiting list, but there was no telling when a place would become available. It could be months or even years.

While Adannaya was contemplating her next course of action, she ran into a fellow school governor who was originally from Morocco in North Africa. His name was Tariq. He was a member of the Labours Party and familiar with educational appeals. Tariq gave Adannaya some tips for her appeal and even went with her to process it, but it made no difference because her appeal still wasn't upheld. Tariq did not give up and came up with another plan.

"You know you can speak to one of the county councillors to raise this issue."

"Really?"

"Yes, because if your daughter experienced racism in a school, it is sufficient reason. You understand?"

"Yes, I understand that, but this school is oversubscribed anyway, and that shaped their response to my appeal. They said it's not that they do not understand my situation, but the issue is that they were oversubscribed. There is no space. So, they have to keep Esther on the waiting list until there is a space. That was the position, not that they didn't want to help," explained Adannaya because she assumed there was no point approaching the school once again

"You know that education sits under the county council, so the county councillors can speak on your behalf as their constituent if you approach them."

Adannaya was still sceptical but had faith in God and believed that He could make a way when there seemed to be no way.

"Okay, why not. If you think it would help."

"I am convinced it would," Tariq reassured her.

He gave Adannaya the contact details of the County Councillor and contacted her. Her name is Sharon. Adannaya explained the situation to her. Sharon was sorry to hear about the racism that Esther experienced. She advised Adannaya on how to draft the right email that could elicit the desired response.

Adannaya wrote the email, and Sharon added her voice and sent it to the education department in the county council. A few days later, they responded that they would investigate it on the basis that the child had experienced racism.

Adannaya assumed that it would take months, but just two weeks later, she received a phone call from the education department. They informed Adannaya that a school place had been found at St Agnes primary school for Esther and that Adannaya was expected at the school to meet the head teacher.

Although St Agnes was not the school Adannaya wanted for Esther, it was a good faith school near her house, so it ticked most of her boxes. She was glad to have a solution to the problem. At last, Esther started at

St Agnes shortly after, and it was all thanks to Tariq and Sharon. It dawned on Adannaya that county councillors were quite influential and did a lot to support families in the community.

Adannaya became friends with Tariq and Sharon. They were both involved in politics in various ways, and they could see that Adannaya would be a fantastic addition to the Labours Party, so they tried to convince her to join them. Tariq kicked it off.

"You are doing really well. You are a parent governor and a trustee governor. The work you are doing at Advent Academy is commendable. Why don't you come and join us? You are the type of people the party is looking for."

"That's right. Someone who is passionate and willing to challenge inequality, advocate for other people, and dogged enough to get to the root of an issue and achieve results for a vulnerable person. You know, no matter how hard it was, you kept on fighting for a place for your daughter. That is the kind of person required in politics," said Sharon persuasively.

Adannaya smiled as she tried to take in what they were saying to her. She could see that others were noticing her hard work and passion for advocacy. Going into politics wasn't something she had ever considered, so she needed to think about it.

"Thank you. I have met Tony Blair, you know. I did volunteer work with a magazine that featured his charitable works, and I attended a few of his conferences. I was captivated by him, and he inspired me. The first time I met him, I was tempted to join the Labours Party, but it wasn't the right time because I needed to focus on settling down in the country.

"Wow! That is amazing," said Tariq, impressed by what Adannaya said.

"Yes, Tony Blair tends to have that effect on people," Sharon nodded knowingly.

"Yes, he does," Agreed Adannaya.

"So, will you join the party?" They both asked her again.

"No problem, I will think about it."

Sharon and Tariq were happy with that.

Adannaya tried to find out more information about politics in the UK. Politics was unfamiliar ground to her. Adannaya's perception of politics was how it was done in Nigeria, which contrasted sharply with the situation in the UK. Back home, it was a game fought with hostility and desperation. It required candidates to invest a lot of their money in the election process, and they did everything possible to win, including bribing voters and election officials.

Adannaya shuddered at the mere thought of being in that political situation. With such thoughts on her mind, Adannaya told Tariq and Sharon that politics was not something she could get involved in. Adannaya was also convinced that she would not have the capacity to be actively involved in politics, considering she was a single mother, full-time student, and school governor.

When they both saw how reluctant Adannaya was and her reasons, they remembered there was an upcoming Beckinghanshire Party women's forum event and secured an invitation for Adannaya.

A few weeks later, Adannaya attended the Women's Forum. Adannaya met a wide range of women. Some were retired, single, married, employed, and unemployed. There were also single mothers, young, old, students, etc. They were such a diverse group of women going by their different categories. What they had in common was that they were all women involved in local government politics in one way or another. There were Councillors and deputy leaders, portfolio holders, local party executives, EXCO members, and role holders in the CLPs. They were all very active people in politics.

Adannaya noticed that there were other women like her whom the Labours Party was trying to win over. There were many presenters and speeches given. When it was over, they asked Adannaya and the other undecided women if they had made up their minds. At that point, Adannaya knew what she wanted to do, and it was to join the Party.

Everyone was happy to hear that, and they promised to provide a lot of support to Adannaya and the new joiners.

Adannaya quickly became an active member of the local Labours Party. She joined them for canvassing at weekends and attended all members' meetings. The first time Adannaya walked into the All-members meeting, she did not see anybody who looked like her, although there were some people from the Asian community. She later found that there were a few black members who were not in the meeting she attended the first time, so she felt a bit different.

On Saturday mornings, when the Constituency Labours Party (CLP) called for volunteers to go canvassing, Adannaya joined them. She dropped Esther off at the supplementary school by the Becking African Caribbean Association. (BACA). The CLP had a clever strategy for canvassing and it was pairing up the newbies with experienced party members.

Adannaya followed them and observed them knocking on doors to speak to people and deliver leaflets. They finished at 1:00 pm, and she picked up Esther afterwards. This became Adannaya's routine, and she continued getting engaged with politics. She became quite confident and good at knocking on doors to speak to strangers.

Adannaya was enjoying the experience and was surprised at how easily she took to politics. It came so easily to her, and she received some positive feedback from her party chairman, Mr Jeff Reid, who said this to her.

"You bring something different to the party. It is not just because you are a black woman; you are a very good team player and have good interpersonal skills. For example, when we go knocking on doors, you are very confident and friendly, speaking with people as though you knew them before. You do not appear fazed by anybody who responds to the doorbell."

"Wow! Thank you, Jeff. This style of politics is all new to me because, as you know, I'm a first-generation migrant. I wasn't born here," said a beaming Adannaya.

"I know, and that's why we welcome that freshness, your friendly and confident attitude on the doorsteps, and your commitment to whatever you are asked to do. The best thing is that you do it all gladly. We notice these things in the party, you know." Jeff assured her. He could see that Adannaya had very strong potential in politics and one that could have a bright future in the party if she wanted it, but he kept that to himself to avoid putting pressure on her.

"Thank you for the feedback and support, Jeff. I appreciate it."

"No worries! You are welcome. My door is always open for any advice on political matters."

"Really? I shall take you up on that offer when I need it."

"Sure. You can count on it."

"Great," said a happy Adannaya.

Adannaya continued to show great commitment to the party as the months went by and never wavered in her efforts and support. During a party fundraising for the parliamentary election, Adannaya made a reasonable donation for the campaign. Many members were impressed. Not only was Adannaya putting in a lot in terms of her time and talent, but she was also making financial contributions. The party started to take notice of Adannaya.

Every year, the party organised local elections because Becking was a 2-tier county council system that divides responsibilities between the county and district councils. When the time for the selection came, many in the party encouraged Adannaya to give it a go, and she agreed to do so. She submitted her application to be included in the CLP candidates for selection.

Following her application, Adannaya was invited to the interview. The interview panel was made up of the EXCO (Executive Committee members of the Becking CLP) and a representative from another CLP. When she arrived, Adannaya realised a few of them knew her, but many of them did not because she was still new to the party.

All candidates were asked the same set of questions during the interview, including whether they had anything to declare that could bring the party to disrepute.

Not only was Adannaya new to Becking but also to politics and the country itself. As with other candidates, at the end of the interview, the panel asked this question,

"Is there anything else you would like to say?"

"I know I am new and don't know Becking very well, but I'm willing to work hard. I'm willing to learn. One thing life has taught me is that no matter where you are, you still need support. I know that because I have been there. So, no matter the situation someone is in, I will be able to understand it because I have once been very successful and have also been vulnerable. I know that being a councillor is about supporting people. No matter where anyone is, I can understand the person, and I will be able to support them."

When Adannaya finished, they asked her to wait outside in the reception area. In less than five minutes, the chairman of the Becking CLP, Jeff Reid, came out to give Adannaya the good news that she had been shortlisted.

"Congratulations, you have been shortlisted. You will now go for selection by the ward members."

"Really? Asked Adannaya in disbelief.

"You passed the interview very well. I have just been given the result, and it was unanimous. What did you say to them?" Asked Jeff curiously.

Adannaya repeated exactly what she said to the panel.

"Well spoken! Now I see why everybody on the panel ticked you off. Pam Pam! Well done"

"Many thanks," smiled Adannaya. She could not believe how quickly it was for the panel to decide. In just five minutes! It was a pleasant surprise!

"You will now move to the next stage of going for your ward selection. So, you're now on the panel of candidates, which means you are eligible for the members to select you."

"Wow, that is good to know."

"The party will now carry out further background checks on you. They will check everything, including your social media accounts" said Jeff.

"Really?"

"Oh yes, they will give you the necessary paperwork to sign at the end of the background checks, so they have the outcome on record."

"Okay, I am happy with that." Adannaya had nothing to hide and no skeletons in her cupboard, so she was happy with that.

"Brilliant!" Nodded Jeff. He hoped Adannaya would win the selection but did not express it.

After Jeff left, Adannaya sat there for a while to take it all in.

Jeff was excited that Adannaya had been certified by the party to become one of the eligible candidates for selection. The reason was that the Labours Party was on the verge of producing the first black female councillor if Adannaya won the election. The election was a by-election for Rallyfield Ward.

Adannaya went through the selection process, which is known as the primaries in Nigeria and other countries. Out of the four candidates for selection, including Adannaya, Adannaya was voted the winner by the members of the Rallyfield ward, and she became the Labours candidate for the ward.

As soon as Adannaya won the selection, her opponents rallied around to support her with the campaign because it was the party fighting the election. It was no longer about the candidate or an individual; it was about the party.

The party started to canvass for votes for the council election and walk the streets of the Rallyfield ward. Adannaya had to juggle campaigning with being a school governor and a student as she was in the final year of her social work programme.

Adannaya knew she wouldn't be able to run for office if the Labours Party had not created an enabling environment that made it possible for women like her to participate in the process. She did not spend a penny of her money on the campaign. The party was responsible for all communication materials for the elections. They had funds available for all expenses. These funds were raised by the party through donations. Remarkably, after the elections, the Election Agent sends an email to ask if there were any expenses incurred during the election so that the receipts could be submitted for reimbursement, even for something as little as the cost of telephone calls.

The party was especially supportive of women, took their childcare constraints into consideration, and, where possible, allowed their female members to bring their children to meetings and conferences. They arranged meetings at suitable times so that women could attend.

In Adannaya's case, the party was flexible in arranging interviews outside of Sunday mornings because they knew her faith was important to her.

The party took all these factors into consideration, especially the fact that Adannaya was a single parent. Her daughter, Esther, was featured in some of her earlier leaflets and newsletters because Adannaya had to take her along, and they ended up being photographed together.

Adannaya worked hard on her campaign, canvassing for votes all over Becking. She spoke to many community groups and received a lot of support.

Adannaya had an interesting occurrence during her campaign. Mrs. Goodluck, the wife of Adannaya's pastor from Nigeria, visited her and offered to join her door-knocking and canvassing. She wanted to experience how local government elections worked in the UK, so they started together.

As Adannaya knocked on doors on one side of the street, her opponent from the other party knocked on the other side of the street. Adannaya exchanged pleasantries with her opponent and wished each other good luck at the polls.

Mrs Goodluck had the mindset of someone coming from Nigeria and was not expecting such civility.

"Ah! Ada, so you mean this is how you do elections in this country?

"Hehehe, yes o!" Adannaya could not contain her laughter at the question, her expression revealing her surprise.

"So, you see your opponent, and you greet each other?"

"That is how we do it here!" Nodded Adannaya

"Wow! Na wa o! In Nigeria, elections are highly competitive and contentious, often marked by strong opposition and significant tension between candidates.

"I know. Don't mind them. That is why women hardly get involved in Nigerian politics," Agreed Adannaya, because she knew the system too well.

They carried on with canvassing as Adannaya knocked on each door and asked for people's votes. Some of them agreed to vote Labours, and others didn't. Adannaya addressed all questions posed and successfully persuaded some individuals to support her candidacy. They continued from street to street and left the campaign leaflets behind.

Chapter 9

DO RALLYFIELD A FAVOUR, VOTE ADANNAYA!

Mrs Goodluck was surprised that Adannaya easily accepted that some of the residents were not going to vote for her.

"Just like that?" She asked. She was shocked beyond words.

"Yes o! At least, I know who will vote for me and who will not," explained Adannaya.

"If it were Nigeria, they would be bribing voters with bags of rice and other things. In fact, there will be a siren or motorcade following you."

Adannaya laughed again as she tried to decide the next street they should canvass for votes. She told Mrs Goodluck how the party took responsibility for all the communication materials for the election and that she did not have to pay a dime from her pocket. That left Mrs Goodluck speechless.

"Ehen! See how the white man organises elections, and everybody respects themselves. What a civilised way of doing elections. When I return to Nigeria, I will tell this story."

"Good. Please tell them. We need to change how we conduct elections over there."

Mrs Goodluck nodded in agreement.

The campaign continued until the day of the election. Adannaya was trained well by her mentor, the CLP chairman, Jeff Reid. She learned that a candidate could lose or win an election in the UK on election day. It was vital for Adannaya to be up at 5:00 a.m. to start delivering leaflets before polling stations opened at 7 am, then later walking the streets, knocking on doors reminding people it was election day, and urging them to go to vote before polls closed at 10:00 pm.

Adannaya's brother, Obioma, arrived two days before the election. He was fascinated by the fact that his sister was running for political office in the UK in such a short time after she arrived here as a broken woman fleeing a bitter and horrible marriage in addition to fighting for her daughter. The transformation and amazing change of circumstances was so sudden and fascinating that Obioma decided to witness it and be there to support his dear sister. Adannaya was grateful for the support because she had no close family in the UK, and having her loving brother there meant a lot to her.

On the night of the election, Obioma was there with her in the counting hall inside the Becking Central Leisure Centre. It was a large hall, and there were many agents counting votes for the different candidates, with the returning officers monitoring the counts as ballot boxes were opened and sorted. It was a frenzied atmosphere with candidates and political parties, media, and the public waiting eagerly for the result of the Rallyfield ward election.

There were 13 candidates, and Adannaya was one of them. She was the only black candidate and immensely proud of her Igbo roots. Adannaya was dressed in her native attire, a lace blouse and George wrapper. She felt she was on the verge of history. All the same, she wondered if she stood a chance against her political opponents in her first election. It was a finger-biting moment as she waited for the votes to be counted and the result announced.

There was a large dark screen above the podium at the front of the hall. The Returning Officer was walking towards the Podium clutching sheets of papers of electoral sensitive materials. The moment of the announcement was approaching, and all eyes were on the dark screen. The Returning officer began to announce the results of each of the thirteen candidates, calling them by names in order of number of votes won.

Adannaya waited anxiously and prayed to her God. The moment came, and to her astonishment, she was announced as the winner, and she won by a huge margin.

COUNCILLOR ADANNAYA MBADIWE HAS BEEN DULY ELECTED

Everyone was clapping and congratulating her. Adannaya stood there beside her brother, Obioma, and she could hear the voices all around her and the smiling faces beaming at her, but her mind went blank. Tears were running down her cheeks uncontrollably because immediately they called her name, something changed automatically inside her. It was an unexplainable feeling. All Adannaya could think about was that she had arrived in the UK not long ago and, within a relatively short period, had become a politician who had just won an election.

Adannaya never imagined that her life's journey would bring her to that point and so quickly too. She had fled Nigeria and arrived in the UK as a broken woman. Coming to the UK gave her this second chance, which took her to a destination that she had never thought possible back home.

It was so surreal that Adannaya wondered if it was true or maybe she was dreaming it all. Then she heard people congratulating her brother, Obioma, and they suddenly nicknamed him 'councillor- brother.' So, it must be real, she thought.

Obioma hugged Adannaya and told her how proud he was of her. Then he whispered into her ear that she should try to compose herself because they were waiting to sign the election acceptance papers.

As Adannaya started the seemingly long but short walk to the podium to sign the acceptance papers, she remembered where she was coming from, and she could not stop her mind from drifting once more to her unique and unusual circumstances—fleeing Nigeria and arriving in the UK a broken woman. She was a woman who was judged by many back home in Nigeria because of her divorce, regardless of all her previous achievements.

In the traditional Igbo society she grew up in, no matter what a woman achieved, she had not achieved much if she was not married. Coming to the UK gave Adannaya a second chance, which was taking her to a destination that she never thought possible because if she were in Nigeria, she would never have dreamt of going into politics. Adannaya was thankful for this opportunity that the UK had given her.

Adannaya continued her walk to the podium to sign the acceptance document. She heard shouts of "Hip hip hooray," and it came from the part of the hall where the Labours Party members were gathered. They were ecstatic that their party had won the election and happy for Adannaya. She smiled at them through her tears and mouthed the words, "Thank you! Thank you very much."

Adannaya looked at the sea of heads in the hall; very few people looked like her. She was the only black candidate and the only black woman out of thirty-six councillors in the council, which really put it into perspective for her. She knew this was not an easy feat to achieve.

Adannaya signed the acceptance papers, and there was even more clapping and a standing ovation led by her mentor and CLP chairman, Jeff Reid. Adannaya was now the newly elected Councillor of Rallyfield ward and the first black person to hold that office.

CHAPTER

10

The First Black Female Councillor

After the election win, there was much celebration in Becking by Adannaya and her friends. The Labours Party was excited to have elected the first black councillor, and the party celebrated in a big way.

The news of Adannaya's victory was very much welcomed back in Nigeria. The family was pleased and pleasantly surprised because, on the one hand, Adannaya had only been in the UK for a short time, and on the other hand, they knew that she had left Nigeria a battered and broken woman. Therefore, to hear that she won the election filled them with joy that she was doing so well, and they were incredibly proud of her.

Her family received the news before Obioma returned home to Nigeria. Adannaya's family and friends posted it all over social media. Akachi was the proudest, telling everyone, "That is my younger sister."

Obioma went home and told the rest of the family the full details of how their sister won the election. Adannaya gave him copies of the ABOUT BECKING monthly magazine with photos of all the elected councillors in Becking. Adannaya Mbadiwe's photo was one of them, and her family was overjoyed to see her listed there. The family celebrated with a family gathering and party.

Adannaya's former GTTNet colleagues were happy to hear of her success. Some did not know she had relocated to the UK and were even more surprised to hear that she had won an election. It seemed quite surprising to them. However, there were a few of her colleagues who already knew she was destined for greatness. One of her colleagues, the head of Public Relations at GTTNet, nicknamed her 'Daughter of Zion.' When he heard the news, he wrote on Facebook that if Adannaya were a man, she would be in Aso Rock (the Nigerian presidential complex), sitting in the cabinet with the president. Adannaya laughed when she read it because she knew being a woman would not stop her from achieving the greatness she was destined for. She knew the hand of God was her and his favour followed her wherever she went in the world.

Regardless of their divorce, Chima also got involved in celebrating Adannaya's success. To him, she was still his wife because her name was still Adannaya Mbadiwe. He printed off the posters of Adannaya's election win from Facebook and posted them on the wall of his business premises.

The Ugwumba family celebrated her victory for quite a while, and her mother was nicknamed 'Mama Honourable,' which she loved. Adannaya was so happy that her mother was alive to see her accomplish this.

Eight months after Adannaya's election win, her beloved mother passed away, and Adannaya travelled to Nigeria for the funeral. Her immediate family, friends, and relatives were already expecting her at NdiOrlu. They were excited to see her, considering there was a funeral and a sad occasion. Her arrival lifted their spirits because of what she had accomplished.

Some of her relatives wanted to know why she used her marital name, Mbadiwe, for the election.

"Well done, our daughter, well done."

"Thank you," said Adannaya.

"We saw your name in the magazine that Obioma brought back. Why are you not using our family name, Ugwumba?" You should be putting the Ugwumba name on the world's map! Change your surname from Mbadiwe," they requested.

"Yes, I plan to change it as soon as I return to the UK," she reassured them.

"We are happy to hear that." They said.

Adannaya was keen to change her surname too, and the only reason she hadn't was that the divorce had not yet been finalised before she ran for election. After the funeral, she went back to Lagos.

Being in Nigeria was like winning the election for the first time all over again. That was because it was what everyone wanted to talk to her about. The congratulatory messages kept coming. Many of Adannaya's friends and former work colleagues got in touch and invited her out to celebrate, and she managed to attend a few.

One of her former colleagues was now a TV presenter, and he invited her for an interview on his show. He said there was a gender equality bill that was being debated in the Senate, and they wanted to know Adannaya's opinion on it. They were also interested to hear how she got into politics and how women were supported in the UK political system compared to Nigeria. Adannaya accepted the television interview, and it was on the prestigious and best private broadcasting station in Nigeria, Channels TV.

Adannaya was happy to talk about the environment that enabled women to participate in politics in the UK and how the parties provided the required support. The presenters on the show were amazed to hear that. They were even more impressed that she navigated the election not only as a new migrant but also as a single mother of a young child.

For the TV interview, she insisted they use her maiden name, Ugwumba, on the caption, not her marital name. Her family saw it when they watched the show, and they were happy and proud to see it because even viewers who did not know who she was recognised the surname and mentioned it to her family members with the same name. Adannaya was making their famous family name even more famous, just like they asked her to. Adannaya was pleasantly surprised at how people at home were celebrating her. She wondered if this is the usual Nigerian celebration of success or if the perception is changing towards divorced and single mothers. Regardless, she enjoyed all the accolades and reconnecting with her family and community again.

When Adannaya returned to the UK, she changed her name to Ugwumba just as she had promised her family and officially notified the Becking Borough Council.

Following the election, a councillor joins various committees, selected in consultation with their political party. In addition, the mayor gifted the councillors the choice of an 'outside organisation 'to be representative of the council. Councillors have a list of organisations to indicate interest, such as the Citizens Advice Bureau, Golf clubs, etc. To her party's surprise, Adannaya did not choose any of the big and prominent organisations. Instead, she chose to be on the board of a church, the Hope Spring church, Becking. It was what Adannaya wanted as her service to God, who had restored and blessed her abundantly and got her to that position.

Hope Spring church was one of the biggest evangelical churches in Becking, and she felt it was a privilege to represent the council on their board regarding the lease arrangements of the premises.

For Adannaya, the best part of being a councillor was the opportunity to advocate for changes that could improve people's lives and represent her constituents. The first motion Adannaya moved was to raise the profile of black history month (BHM) celebrations in Becking, and she won, although Adannaya was an opposition councillor in Becking. This was significant because it was unanimously agreed.

Adannaya was congratulated by her fellow councillors and the community. The Labours Party celebrated the motion, which was widely covered by local newspapers and social media. Her party made a splash of it by raising their profile to elect the first black councillor in Becking, who was already achieving great feats. Adannaya was still new to her role as a councillor, so winning this motion helped boost her confidence.

Since then, the organisation of the Black History Month celebration has improved significantly. BACA now has a website and a dedicated committee that organises events promoting black excellence and culture in Becking, much to the delight of the black community. It is now a month-long event throughout October, and it was all thanks to Adannaya's motion.

Councillor Adannaya Ugwumba became even more popular in Becking, and members of her Rallyfield ward could easily contact her. There were various requests for help, which were known as casework. Some were about housing, education, waste collection, etc. Adannaya was happy to pick up this casework because it meant she could advocate increasingly for more people.

A particular case in which she was notable was the request to intervene to support a student on the verge of expulsion from a secondary school. The student's mother, Mrs Okonkwo, contacted Adannaya and arranged a meeting with the headteacher and deputy headteacher at school. When Adannaya and Mrs Okonkwo arrived at the school, Adannaya was taken aback by the fact that the white headteacher and her deputy could not attempt to pronounce the name of the boy properly. His first name was an Igbo name, Chimfurumnanya, but they also pronounced it Chieflana and spelled it like that. Adannaya could not ignore it and had to intervene.

"Who is this Chieflana you are referring to?" She asked the headteacher.

"That is the name of the boy, isn't it?" Asked the headteacher.

"No, that is not my son's correct name, and I have informed the school several times." Answered Mrs Okonkwo.

"Please, can we just make some attempt to write his name correctly and try to pronounce it correctly too?" Requested Adannaya politely.

"We apologise for that, but some of these names are quite difficult to pronounce with an English accent like ours," explained the deputy headteacher.

"I can understand that, but how do you explain misspelling the name?" queried Adannaya.

“Whenever I see my son’s exam results, it looks like it belonged to someone else” said Mrs Okonkwo.

“Exactly!” Nodded Adannaya. This proves my point. That exam result could be rejected on the grounds that it doesn’t belong to Chimfurumnanya.”

“We see what you mean,” nodded the headteacher.

“We will get it corrected,” promised the deputy head-teacher.

“Thank you. The beauty of African names is that they come with a lot of history and the story of the circumstances of the birth of the child. It is part of a child’s identity. It is not just a name. It is the story of an entire community sometimes. Actually, Chimfurumnanya means ‘My God loves me.’

“Wow! I never knew that.” Smiled the headteacher in surprise.

“I guess that is why they say there is something in a name,” agreed the deputy headteacher.

Adannaya was glad that they understood the point she was trying to make, and she continued.

“So that is why it is important for these names to be pronounced properly and written correctly.”

“Noted,” chorused the headteacher and her deputy as they made notes about it.

The meeting continued, and Adannaya was able to resolve the difficulty that put the child at risk of expulsion. Her intervention made Adannaya even more popular because Mrs Okonkwo and her husband told anyone who would listen how amazing Adannaya was. Not only was their son not expelled from school, but she also resolved their ongoing misunderstanding with the school over the mispronunciation and misspelling of their son's name.

Adannaya was growing as a councillor and making a great difference in the lives of her ward members. Her mentor, Jeff Reid, gave her good references to apply for leadership training to further develop and hone her political skills. Adannaya applied for the Jo Cox Women in Leadership Programme and Fabian Women Network Mentoring Programme.

They were extremely competitive, and to be accepted is something to celebrate because they selected about fifty women across the country each year.

The Jo Cox training provided the necessary skills in public speaking and campaigning. During the training, participants were tasked with developing a TED talk on any subject of their choice, which they will present to their colleagues and facilitators for feedback. Adannaya was able to deliver a TED talk titled 'Second Class Citizen: A Sequel" which received applause. It was based on the book by her favourite author, Buchi Emecheta, titled *Second Class Citizen*.

As part of the programme, Adannaya was assigned a mentor who was a member of parliament (an MP). Her mentor invited her for a tour of the House of Parliament in Westminster. During the tour, she heard about the Women Suffragists **Millicent Fawcett** and Emily Davidson, who fought for Parliament to give women over 21 the right to vote in 1928. Adannaya reflected that she was standing on the sacrifice of these women who paved the way for women like her. She visited the chapel in the parliament and knelt and prayed there, thanking her God for bringing her this far.

Adannaya participated in the Fabian Women Mentoring programme, which took her to the devolved nations of the United Kingdom, where she visited the Scottish and Welsh Assembly to learn about local government and devolution matters.

Adannaya moved another motion that was crucial. The motion was to ban the marketing of vaping products to children. She was one of the very few councillors to move this motion, which later became a national debate.

Adannaya was inspired to move the motion due to a personal experience. She went with her 14-year-old daughter, Esther, and her friend to one of the phone repair shops. Adannaya stayed in the car and asked her daughter to go across the road and pick up the phone, which had been submitted for repairs a few days prior. When Esther came out of the phone shop, she said to her mum:

"Mummy, the person in the store asked me if I would like to buy vapes."

"What?" She was appalled at what she just heard, so she quickly got out of the car and went inside the phone shop with Esther and her friend.

The customer service assistant was a young man. Adannaya queried him.

"Why are you marketing vapes to my daughter?"

"I thought she was sixteen. They buy it all the time."

"She is not sixteen, and even if she was, did she ask you for a vape?" Demanded Adannaya.

"Okay, sorry," he said.

"From today, please stop marketing vapes to children because you are breaking the law."

Adannaya left that phone shop thinking about the vaping problem in the community, especially with regard to children. Working with schools, she knew schools were struggling to confiscate vapes as children were hiding in the toilet to smoke because where there were no smoke alarms in there.

Also working with NHS as a Child Adolescent Mental Health Services (CAMHS) senior manager, she knew there was yet no scientific evidence regarding the impact of vapes on young people. Vaping was encouraged for adults who were already smokers and wanted to quit smoking. It was not meant for children to smoke for the fun of it. Adannaya recognized the need for clarity on how it is marketed and used and the importance of educating about its potential impact on young minds. Based on that, she brought the motion to the council.

The majority party in the Becking council (the Democrats) were interested in the motion and asked for an amendment to make it a joint motion because they knew that she was going to win the motion. Adannaya and her party accepted the amendment, and she moved it as a joint motion. It was agreed unanimously. It was an exciting news item.

Becking Observer Newspaper picked it, and so did the Beckinghanshire Gazette. They splashed it on the local news. Local radio stations reached out to Adannaya, and she participated in several interviews where she explained her motivations for proposing the motion.

Other councillors outside Adannaya's party and region contacted her for permission to replicate her motion in their council, which she gladly gave. Within a short time, the topic was a national agenda debated in the House of Parliament. Legislation on marketing vaping products to children was tightened as a result.

One of the highlights of Adannaya's tenure as a councillor was the opportunity to attend a party at Buckingham Palace. It was the Royal Garden party to celebrate the coronation of King Charles.

Adannaya was excited to receive the email that she had been nominated to attend. She had only visited Buckingham Palace as a tourist and never dreamed she would be able to enter the palace one day. Adannaya felt incredibly blessed by her God once again. The invitation advised that Adannaya could attend the event with her consort, and she took her good friend, Chief Okwuchi.

On the day of the Royal Garden party, Adannaya and her consort were dressed in full Nigerian traditional attire to the delight of the other non-ethnic guests who kept asking what the feathers on Chief Okwuchi's red cap symbolised, and he gladly told them. There were so many people invited to the event. People who had done well in the community and those who were also nominated, not just politicians. Adannaya met a lot of people from diverse sectors, including the military, public, and voluntary sectors. There were people from all the nations of the United Kingdom: England, Scotland, Wales, and Northern Ireland.

Adannaya met Prince William, the Prince of Wales, Princess Kate, and the Princess Royal, Princess Anne, who rode in on her horse. Prince William addressed them and interacted with many of them.

The food served was tea, drinks, and cakes. Adannaya was surprised at the food and found it funny that it was just tea, drink, and cakes. Where she came from in Nigeria, if a king invited you to a banquet, the table would be full of a large variety of cooked food. It was clearly different in the UK.

Although they enjoyed the scrumptious cakes, Adannaya and her consort were still hungry when they left the royal garden party, so they headed straight for the nearest Nigerian restaurant to enjoy their favourite native Igbo cuisine.

Adannaya was an excellent councillor and continued to accomplish remarkable outcomes for her residents as a ward Councillor. She continued to grow in the party and build her political muscle. Adannaya rose to become the deputy group leader for the group following an election by her fellow councillors. This made her the first black female deputy group leader in the group. This boosted Adannaya's profile and gave her even more exposure; she could speak at regional and national conferences.

CHAPTER 11

The First Citizen

Another election season came around, and Adannaya started preparing for it as she became familiar with the end-to-end election process. She was selected once again by the Labours Party to stand for Rallyfield Ward.

Adannaya's amazing performance as a councillor in the community made her well-known, and she received a lot of support from the community through her campaign. Many people joined her for leafleting, door knocking, designing and printing flyers, etc.

On the election day, everyone gathered at the election hall once again. As usual, it was a pensive atmosphere. The returning officers briefed the Labours Party agent that the votes were too close to call and that they were going to do a recount. When the agent told Adannaya about it, her heart sank.

She knew the Democrats were desperate to win Rallyfield Ward for their party, and they threw all they had into it. They brought the party big wigs and high-profile members to walk all the streets and canvass for votes.

Before that moment, Adannaya was sure she would be re-elected based on her excellent performance during her first tenure. That certainty suddenly disappeared, and she became worried about the outcome of the election.

The bad news came eventually, and her mentor, Jeff Reid, informed Adannaya that she lost the election by twenty-five votes. The returning officer announced exactly that. Adannaya was devastated by the hard it. Her party members were shocked to hear that she had lost the election, and they commiserated with her. Adannaya thanked them all and went home.

Losing the election did not stop Adannaya from carrying on with her work in the Labours Party because she knew it was just a setback. As every politician knew, another opportunity would present itself for re-election, and when that time came, Adannaya would be ready for it. In the meantime, she became even more valuable to the CLP by immersing herself in the running of the local party. Her dedication paid off, and the party members elected her as the vice-chairman of the CLP, the first black woman to hold that position. She served alongside her mentor, Jeff Reid, who was the chairman of the CLP.

After two years, one of the councillors in another ward in Becking, (Kamwood ward) gave notice that she was going to retire at the end of her tenure. This meant another councillor had to be elected to replace her, and the permutation around that began. The seat was a safe Labours seat, and that generated a lot of interest because everyone knew that any Labours candidate would most likely win that seat.

Adannaya put in her application for selection. After the usual interview, four candidates were eventually shortlisted. Three of the candidates lived in the Kamwood ward, and Adannaya was the only candidate living outside the ward. She knew how hard it was going to be because she was not well known in the ward compared to her competitors. The three other candidates knew all the members living in the ward.

Adannaya intensified her effort as though she was campaigning for the council election instead of a selection contest. She spoke to all the active members individually and wrote to each of them. She shared her manifesto with them and her past achievements as a councillor in Rallyfield, especially the motions she moved. Some of them knew who she was because they had encountered her in her role as a social worker in Becking. This was certainly a plus because her excellent social work and advocacy in the community spoke for her.

On the day of the selection, each candidate had ten minutes to address the members. Adannaya chose to go first because she wanted to set the tone for the selection. She blew them away with her speech because her previous experience made it easy for her to know exactly what to say at times like this. It was a hard-fought contest, and the other candidates were prepared as well.

Adannaya's speech and campaign must have been very convincing because she emerged as the winner with over 50% of the votes. The result of the vote was a surprise to her, considering there were three candidates. Adannaya was ecstatic and grateful to God for making it possible. She became the Labours candidate for Kamwood ward.

The election came, and Adannaya did not take her expected victory for granted. Just because Kamwood Ward was a Labours Party stronghold did not mean she shouldn't fight for every vote. She campaigned hard as usual and received a lot of support from the community with her campaign. It paid off, and Adannaya won the election with a margin of over sixty percent. It was another happy and memorable occasion for Adannaya, her party, as well as her friends and family.

Adannaya went right back to supporting and advocating for her community. She supported another motion, and this time, it was to increase diversity by improving street naming in Becking, and the motion passed. It was a type of motion that required a task force. The council agreed on this but needed someone to chair the task force. Since the Democratic Party were the leading party in the council, they chaired most committees and task forces in the council. Adannaya decided to apply for the role; after all, it was her party that raised the motion.

Adannaya beat the Democratic party candidate and became the chairman of the task force. She successfully led the task force, and it launched her further into the community because she led it in a different way by inviting community leaders to the task force to share their views on the matter. Following the recommendation of the task force, the Council named a new street in Becking after a black ex-footballer, and the name's now ISA YARO Street. He was the perfect person for this honour because he was a much-loved and celebrated footballer in Becking. This was the successful outcome of the cross-party task force Adannaya chaired.

After chairing the task force amazingly, the following year, Adannaya became Vice chairman of the overview and scrutiny committee. The role was a very important position to have because the committee scrutinised decisions made by the cabinet and council in the borough, including outsourced services.

Adannaya was growing even more in the political arena and attended national and regional conferences. She resigned from her position as the vice chair of the CLP and once again became deputy group leader of the councillors. Adannaya moved a joint motion with the Democrats once again, and this time, it was focused on challenging violence against women and girls. The motion passed, and Becking became a white ribbon council, which meant that council key officials and councillors are allies and advocates for women's safety. These achievements increased Adannaya's visibility, and she continued to advance in the council.

Every year, the Becking council selected who would be the next mayor of Becking. First, the councillors elected one of their fellow councillors to be deputy mayor. Whoever became the deputy mayor would take over from the incumbent mayor to become mayor the following year.

The Labours Party had ten councillors, while the Democratic Party had twenty-six councillors. Each Councillor could nominate themselves for the position of deputy mayor. The eligibility criteria included that the councillor's tenure will not end in the period required to serve as mayor and not be a cabinet member.

Adannaya had put herself forward for the nomination a couple of times, but she never made it because the councillors seemed to vote along party lines. Therefore, the Labours Party candidate usually ended up with a far smaller number of votes than the Democratic candidate. It was a no brainier. Politics is a game of numbers.

After two attempts, Adannaya almost gave up trying, but due to her usual doggedness, she decided to try one more time. This particular year, and as fate would have it, no councillor from the Democratic put in a nomination before the deadline, so they lost their chance. Even a last-minute candidate (after the deadline) was not eligible . This unique circumstance made her nomination successful. Adannaya believed that this was God intervening in her life once again to make the seemingly impossible possible for her.

Adannaya became the only candidate standing for the position of deputy mayor. When she was presented to the full council for approval, their decision was unanimous. They had seen how effective she was as a councillor and serving in various capacities, and they knew she would be an excellent mayor. Adannaya was elected unopposed as the deputy mayor of Becking.

Adannaya's year as deputy mayor was a busy one because she deputised for the mayor and attended many civic events. She balanced her responsibilities as the ward councillor of Kamwood ward, her role as an NHS senior manager, and several other duties. Nevertheless, she enjoyed it immensely, and it was a good preparation for when she became the mayor.

The mayor of a council is THE FIRST CITIZEN of the Borough. It is a very important position, and the council usually organises a special inauguration ceremony to transfer the office from the departing mayor to the incoming one. It was going to be the peak of Adannaya's political career as a councillor, and she was determined to celebrate it as best she could.

Adannaya set up a planning committee with her friends and leaders of the various communities to support the planning of the celebration event that would take place after the inauguration ceremony. It was going to be the biggest civic event and celebration of the year in Becking.

Adannaya was looking forward to the inauguration ceremony, and so were her family members. Some of her siblings planned to travel down from the USA and Nigeria to attend the ceremony. Her cousins in Italy were also coming. It was going to be a very exciting event. Adannaya ordered the most beautiful Nigerian attire from Lagos, Nigeria, for the event.

On the day of the inauguration, Becking council was buzzing with excitement. It was so colourful because of the rich and diverse culture of the Becking community. Adannaya had touched the communities; Asian. African, Caribbean, Arabian, Jewish, English, Irish, Polish, Romanians, Portugues, etc. They all turned up in large numbers to celebrate and honour her. It was a historic occasion that the first African was about to become mayor of Becking.

Adannaya entered the inauguration hall in all her glory, and the ceremony started. She was accompanied by her consort, Chief Okwuchi. Her family members, friends, and key representatives of the Becking community were all seated. They all looked spectacularly gorgeous in their beautiful clothes. The mace holder walked in with the mace at 6:30 pm. The current mayor stepped down after a speech. Adannaya walked up to the podium and was handed the mace of office to rapturous applause. She made a speech, and it was her best ever:

"I would like to express my deepest appreciation to everyone for making out time to honour me today at this epic event. We made history ten years ago when you elected me as the first African councillor in Becking Council. Today, we have raised the flag higher by inaugurating me as the first African to become the mayor of Becking. Our Borough continues to be the trailblazer in Beckinghanshire for promoting inclusion and celebrating the strength in the diversity of our community. As you can see, ever since my election, the make-up of Becking councillors continues to reflect the population it serves."

There was loud applause and a standing ovation. She smiled and mouthed the words, "Thank you! Thank you!" Adannaya had to pause until it died down before she continued.

"I am humbled and honoured to be your First Citizen. When I was a little girl in secondary school in Nigeria, I read a book titled, *Second Class Citizen* by the award-winning author, Buchi Emechtta. I said to myself then that when I grew up, I would write the sequel to this book, and the title would be 'First Class Citizen.' Little did I know I would become 'The First Citizen.' I am grateful to God and all of you for making my dreams a beautiful reality today despite the twists and turns of my life journey.

There was more applause, and Adannaya had to pause once again.

"The theme for my tenure is 'Togetherness.' This will be reflected in all the Civic events and community engagements we shall carry out together in the coming year. My mission is to showcase the beautiful and diverse communities that make Becking unique, thereby promoting connections and togetherness. I have chosen to support three charities that reflect my passion during my tenure. Being a social worker, I am passionate about improving outcomes for young people. As a result, the first charity I am announcing today is the *Becking Youth Project.* My second charity is *Becking Cancer Support.* It reflects my passion for raising awareness and supporting people living with cancer in our diverse communities.

"My third charity is *Becking Forever Community,* which aligns with my commitment to promoting mental health awareness and early intervention within our community.

The applause was deafening this time, and there were shouts of "Yes! Yes!" and "Thank you! Thank you". Adannaya knew that many would relate to those charities, and she was right. She grinned.

"Thank you too because I seem to have chosen the right charities, which means I can look forward to seeing many of you during the various fun fundraising events we shall organise to support the work of these charities. I also like to let you know there is more celebration in the horizon as I just received communication that I have been nominated for the Brunie University Alumni of the Year Award.

I invite you to work with me to showcase Becking to the world together. Remember, we are not just any Borough. We are Becking!

"We are bold!

We are strong!

We are ambitious!

We are innovative!

"Thank you everyone for coming"

Okwuchi	God's word
Sade	Honour earns a crown
Tufuakwa	Exclamation for Abomination
Ugwumba	The pride of the town
Yaro	Boy
Yusuf	God increases

Emeka	Short form of Chukwuemeka (God has done exceedingly well)
Ewo	Exclamation of Surprise
Eziokwu	True
Isa	Islamic version of the Christian name 'Isaac'
Ko ni da fuen	Woe betide you
Lolo	A wife with a title or Wife of a titled man
Mazi	Mr
Mbadiwe	The Town is desperate
Mbanu	Disagree
Mechie onu	Keep quiet
Nau	Pidgin English for the word 'Now'
Ngozi	Blessing
Nkechi	God's own
Nne	Mother (Also a pet name for fe-male)
Nwanneka	Sibling Relationship is supreme
Obioma	Kind Heart
Obidiya	Her husband's heart
Ogechi	God's time
Oliseh	God
Okafor	Male child born on Afor day
Okeke	Male born on Eke day
Okey	Short form for Okechukwu-My portion from God
Okonkwo	Male child born on Nkwo day

Okwuchi	God's word
Sade	Honour earns a crown
Tufuakwa	Exclamation for Abomination
Ugwumba	The pride of the town
Yaro	Boy
Yusuf	God increases